th type taster

How fonts influence you
By Sarah Hyndman

type
tasting®

The type taster: How fonts influence you

Published by Type Tasting

Limited first edition of 2,000

© 2015 Sarah Hyndman

The main body of this book is written in *Franklin Gothic*, which I chose because it is a readable classic. Styles like this were used for early American tabloid newspaper headlines and this gives it a populist undertone which reminds me not to take myself too seriously.

The large titles are in *Balega* which is a solid, chunky display face with curves and points that give it character; it looks interesting and feels a little challenging.

I chose *Monotype Century Expanded* for the notes and picture captions because this is a traditional serif typeface that feels knowledgeable.

Courier Sans is used for instructions and data because it is based on the Macintosh system font (but with its serifs cut off) and its open letters feel clear and uncomplicated.

Franklin Gothic was originally designed by Morris Fuller Benton in 1902. *Balega* was designed by Jürgen Weltin in 2003. *Monotype Century Expanded* was designed by Linn Boyd Benton in conjunction with T. L. DeVinne in 1894. *Courier Sans* was designed by James Goggin between 1994 and 2001.

Written and designed by Sarah Hyndman

Printed by L&S Printing

Thank you to Monotype for the fonts

To Tina F-P and Mum for your tenacity and inspiration.

drink me

drink me

Eat
Me

Diet food

Eat
Me

Instant

EAT
ME

economy

Eat
Me

Decadent

PHRENOLOG
BY
L.N. FOWLER

FORTUNE TELLER

Bodoni

Miracle Font

Pick a font to reveal your fortune

FORTUNE TELLER

Bauhaus

Miracle Font

Pick a font to reveal your fortune

FORTUNE TELLER

Gill Sans

Miracle Font

Pick a font to reveal your fortune

FORTUNE TELLER

Caslon

Miracle Font

Pick a font to reveal your fortune

Contents

Who is this book for?

Fonts are no longer just for 'geeks' and graphic designers. Thanks to technology and the gadgets we use, more people than ever before are aware of them—from gateway fonts* like *Comic Sans* to the superstar typefaces like *Helvetica* and *Gotham*.

We are all type consumers. Typefaces/fonts play a vital role in our everyday lives. They help us to navigate, to make choices, to shop, they keep us safe and sometimes they play a game of sleight of hand.

This book is for you if:

- You are a type consumer who would like to be more aware of fonts and how you are influenced by them.

- You work in the technology and communication industries and want to know more about the power of type.

- You are a graphic designer, or design student who would like to read a book on typography that takes a different approach including research and current thinking.

In this book you are invited to consider your emotional response to type. Each font or typeface has a personality that influences your interpretation of the words you are reading, by evoking your emotions and setting the scene. You instinctively understand this, but it happens on a subconscious level. Becoming consciously aware of the emotional life of fonts can be entertaining and ultimately give you more control over decisions you make.

*Applying gateway drug theory to typography is to suggest that using a seemingly naive font could open the door to the use of more serious and 'hard core' typefaces.

About the author

Sarah Hyndman set up Type Tasting on Valentine's Day 2013 with an evening of Typographic Swearing 'n' Cussing. Type Tasting is based on the idea of wine tastings and it is a forum for discussions, research, and to learn about the experience of consuming type. The approach is to do this in an entertaining and inspiring way which opens out the conversation beyond the design world.

Since the launch, Sarah has organised and curated a mass participation typography exhibition and run workshops at the Victoria and Albert Museum (V&A) for the London Design Festival. She has been interviewed on BBC Radio 4's 'Today' and 'The Arts Hour', participated in 'Pick Me Up' at Somerset House and created edible type for Monotype. Sarah has talked about Type Tasting at South by Southwest (SXSW) in Austin, Texas and has given a TEDx talk called 'Wake Up and Smell the Fonts'. She runs workshops for the D&AD, is working on collaborative research with the Crossmodal Research Laboratory at Oxford University and is writing her next book for Laurence King Publishing.

Before setting up Type Tasting Sarah ran her own design company, With Relish, which she started in 2003 with clients including the Almeida Theatre, London and Coutts. Sarah completed a masters degree in Typo/Graphics at the London College of Communication in 2001. She was subsequently invited back as a guest tutor to set up and run the year-long Experimental Typography evening course, which she did for six years alongside her commercial practice.

Sarah is available for type tastings, talks and workshops. These range from intensive, creative workouts for designers to enlightening and entertaining sessions for non-designers which are all created to be fun and accessible with a twist of theatre.

Find out more at typetasting.com

Links to the organisations mentioned can be found on page 140.

Introduction

I first fell in love with type in the 1970s as a child in a sweetshop on the way home from school. Here, unlike in the classroom where I read 'serious' typefaces, words came to life as they fizzed and popped with excitement all shouting out their different flavours. I realised that fonts are like multisensory imagination grenades.

I have now been a graphic designer for almost 20 years. I began working in big agencies where I learned about the power of type and then I set up my own design company in 2003.

This book takes you through the findings of my journey of discovery that started two years ago when I turned the tables on myself and set off to explore fonts from the type consumer's (or user's) point of view.

It has been important for me to talk to as many people as possible along the way which has involved running events, inventing games, giving talks, getting out of the graphic design world and asking lots of questions. I have read research dating back to the 1920s and, where I cannot find proven answers, I have run experiments and created my own surveys. These have been designed to gather data but also to be fun and to get people thinking about fonts.

This curiosity has opened up new avenues that I could not have imagined, like working with scientists at Oxford University to explore how type can influence our senses.

The stories and discoveries in this book are my personal observations and are based on my experiences. As a graphic designer I am a generalist which means I try to take a wide viewpoint and gather information from a variety of sources. As with everything else I do, this book is intended as a conversation starter.

1

"Typefaces, they don't really matter?"

Justin Webb, BBC Radio 4 *Today*

Dalston Type Safari
Sign painted 'Mockingbird Tapas & Cocktails' / Art Deco 'Jazz Bar' / New York style 'Voodoo Ray's' / Blackletter 'Ta' / Fried chicken shop Flare Serif 'S' / 'Moustache Bar' icon / 70s style 'G' in *Candice* / Vernacular 'Tom's Bakery' / New York style 'Voodoo Ray's' 'S' / Art Deco 'R' / 'Dalston Superstore' in neon / 'Ruby's' sign in condensed *Helvetica* / Mosaic lettering / 'Crown and Castle' Grotesque Sans Serif / Geometric 'Dalston Culture House' / Woodblock inspired 'Birthday's' 'B'.

"TYPEFACES, THEY DON'T REALLY MATTER?"

I was sitting nervously in the BBC Radio 4 'Today' studio very early one Saturday morning trying hard not to think about the 'seven million listeners' as I was about to do my first ever live radio interview. Time was slowing down and my heartbeat was getting louder as I waited the eternity it seemed to take for the interview to begin. As the moment got closer I started to worry that, not only was I losing the ability to speak, but also I could no longer remember anything—not even my name. How was I ever going to have a conversation about typefaces?

Finally the light saying 'live' went on and the interviewer turned to me and said "Typefaces, they don't really matter?"[1] This is a question that I have been asked so many times that I forgot my nerves and found myself taking on the familiar role of 'type advocate' as we chatted about the importance of type in our everyday lives.

Type consumers

We are all type consumers: we all interact with, and consume, a vast array of typefaces every day of our lives and most of the time we do this without being consciously aware of it. Type influences what we read and affects our choices because we all instinctively understand what it is communicating to us, and we have been learning to interpret the references all our lives.

As a graphic designer I actively think about type when I am working but once I am 'off duty' I become a type consumer. At this point I generally stop paying attention to fonts. Occasionally I will notice one if it stands out for a reason; I might find it particularly pleasing, unexpected or an inappropriate choice.

I was interested to see how many fonts I consume as I go about my everyday life, so I set myself the challenge of counting how many I encountered over the course of an hour on a Saturday morning.

Phone: check time, emails (2) / Bathroom: toothpaste, shower products, toiletries (7) / Open curtains: road markings, signs, vehicles (3) / Kitchen: coffee, fridge, clock (5) / Breakfast ingredients (7) / Toaster, microwave (3) / Living room: TV, news, advertisements (14) / Sort through books and magazines, pick a bag up off the floor (7) / Computer (5) / Items on the desk (4) / Open post (9) / **Total: 67**

This takes a bit of focus as you quickly forget to notice the fonts and get distracted by the activities. Try this challenge for yourself. How many fonts do you consume in an hour?

Curating fonts

Famous brand logos can often be recognised from the type alone. What you see can be reduced down to just a fragment of the logo and you will still know instantly what the brand is. This is because your brain is a 'pattern-matching machine'. You compare what you look at to things you have seen before and catalogued in your mind. Once a logo has become familiar you no longer even need to read the words to know what they say, because you recognise it by its shape: think about the Coca-Cola or Google logos. You do this from an early age which is demonstrated well by Anna, aged 4, whose mother Sandra tweeted "Our daughter Anna says our car is from Boots (the chemist). What is our car?" The answer is on page 21.

We curate the logos we surround ourselves with from the brands we use in our everyday rituals. These range from toothpaste and shampoo, the objects that we select to reflect our personality like the brands of clothes that we wear, to expensive lifestyle items like cars. We are "creatures of habit" says design writer Steven Heller[2] who observes that it takes a "diabolically brilliant" marketing plan to entice us to change our brand loyalty. But if a brand alters its typography to a style that no longer feels in keeping with our values we can be acutely aware of the change. In 2010 high street fashion shop Gap scrapped its redesign after just a few days following customer protests that the new logo looked "cheapy, tacky, ordinary" and returned to the original logo created from the *Spire* typeface.[3]

Original design: *Spire*

Redesign: *Helvetica bold*

Game: Supermarket Sweep

Congratulations you've won the lottery! To celebrate you're going to buy all the luxury items in the shop. How long will it take you to find all the luxury products?

Supermarket A

Number of luxury items:

Time taken to find them:

Now turn the page to go to Supermarket B.

Font users

After centuries of having typefaces chosen for us by designers and printers, we now live in a time where design tools are being increasingly democratised and more people than ever before are finding themselves looking down a font menu and deciding which ones to choose.

At a recent event I asked a 12-year-old for her thoughts on the typefaces I had printed out on a table for a game. I was taken aback by how articulately she explained which she would choose for different genres of books. She told me that she would change the font on her Kindle until it "felt right" for each book she read. She preferred *Palatino* for fiction set in the past and *Futura* for her factual schoolbooks. The other youngsters in the room said they went through a similar process. When I was a child the typeface was an immutable part of a book because the designer or printer had already selected it. Since I had no choice I took typefaces for granted. Having a choice has given today's young people a new appreciation of type, and selecting a font has become as normal as choosing which t-shirt to wear or which cereal to have for breakfast.

Fonts save you time

Imagine a world with just one typeface? This might be an aesthetically appealing idea if you picture a 1950s shop full of packaging with type all neatly lined up in a clean, Sans Serif style like *Helvetica*. This is the design of supermarket A (above). However the reality is that, although this shop might look stylish and relaxing, your shopping trip would take much longer without the extensive visual clues typefaces give you. You would have to stop and read the words on every pack to find out

Supermarket B

Number of luxury items:

Time taken to find them:

See page 21 for the answers. It should have taken you considerably less time to find the luxury items in supermarket B where the typefaces give you visual clues.

whether it is a luxury or a cheap product, the full fat or healthy option, your favourite brand, that one you would never buy or your guilty pleasure.

Fonts help you to choose

Typefaces help you to decide who you would trust to do a professional job for you. For example which of these three lawyers would you hire? (See page 57).

LAWYER

LAWYER

Lawyer

(a)   (b)   (c)

The
Ampersand
Arms

(d)

The
Ampersand
Arms

(e)

&

**The
Ampersand
Arms**

(f)

When you are in a new town the signs over the doors help you to choose where to eat and drink. Which of the three 'The Ampersand Arms' on the left do you think would suit you and why? (See page 133). However, the signs can occasionally be misleading: for example, there is a pub I walk past regularly with a sign in an Ornate Script similar to example (e). This is a style you are used to seeing on wine labels and wedding invitations, so you could assume that it is a wine bar or somewhere to go for a quiet, romantic drink. The reality is quite the opposite as you, in fact, find yourself in a noisy, beer drinkers' pub with people standing around watching football on the large television screens.

Fonts keep you safe

When driving you need to know instantly whether a sign is official and you must react quickly, or whether it is simply an advert that you can read at

Clearview	
Frutiger	Serif to Sans Serif
Helvetica	

Destination: Paris
Art Nouveau, eg *Arnold Boecklin*

Destination: London
Johnston is the official London Transport typeface

DESTINATION: NEW YORK
Geometric sans serif eg *Twentieth Century*

your leisure (or choose to ignore). Official road signs fit an established set of visual conventions. They use clear and neutral type which is highly readable, and generally in a Sans Serif style because these have proved to be the most readable from a distance in tests.

The road sign system in Britain was created in the 1960s by Jock Kinneir and Margaret Calvert[4] who designed the two new typefaces *Transport* and *Motorway* as part of the project. Life-sized signs were made and tested for readability in an underground car park and in London's Hyde Park. Kinneir and Calvert established that words set in upper and lower case are more legible than those in just upper case as they have silhouettes which can be distinguished from a distance. This was considered controversial at the time.

By contrast the advertising signs which sit alongside the road signs shouting out their messages can easily be distinguished by their decorative and colourful letters, each with their own brand type style, colour and images (above).

Fonts show you the way...

Official directional signs in a visually cluttered and busy airport are generally easy to recognise, even when you are in unfamiliar surroundings or the signs are in a different language. According to design writer Alissa Walker[5] there are just three typefaces used by around three quarters of the airports in the world: *Clearview*, *Frutiger* and *Helvetica* (above). These are chosen for their clarity and readability and are similar in style to the type found on road signs.

... and tell you where you are

Once you have arrived at your destination, you know immediately if you are in another country from the less familiar style of lettering on the signs and businesses. In Paris the influences of Art Nouveau can still be widely seen, for example, on the Metro signs. The unofficial typeface of London is *Johnston* which is used across the London transport system. Geometric Sans Serif styles like *Twentieth Century* were popular on signage in New York in the mid-20th century and these inspired Tobias Frere-Jones' *Gotham* typeface which was made famous when it was used for Obama's 2008 presidential campaign.

If you were to be parachuted into an unknown location it is the content and style of the signage that would give you some of the biggest clues to your whereabouts. You can test this out by playing the online game GeoGuessr.com,[6] which transports you to a random location somewhere in the world using Google Streetview. The challenge is to see how quickly you can work out where you are.

Typographic DNA

The combination of type found on signage reveals a great deal about a city, town or specific area. It reflects the social, economic and historical development of the area and creates its own, unique typographic DNA.

I take people on Type Safaris through Dalston in East London. These are guided walks exploring the signage with a photography challenge to take part in along the way. We usually end by having drinks in a quintessentially 'Dalston style' bar which has a checkered lino floor (from its previous life as a furniture shop), a glitter ball and lampshades made from plastic colanders.

Dalston is a vibrant area that has undergone dramatic change since the East London rail line

was extended to the area. The signs along the main road, Kingsland Road, reveal layers of history dating back to when it was a London outpost in the 1800s. Signs from the Art Deco cinemas have been preserved alongside the vernacular D.I.Y. signage of the market stalls and the lettering over the shops and restaurants that reflect the different communities who have made the area home over the years. More recent additions are the trendy bars and shops as the area has become popular with artists and students and it is now an established social destination. Venues continue to pop up and vanish, often retaining the signage and the name of their previous incarnations during their fleeting lifespans.

Type Safari challenge

Take up the challenge and create a typographic composition to reflect the area where you live.

1. Think of a phrase, quote, memory or lyric that you associate with the area, ideally between 10 and 25 characters long (including spaces).

2. Write this down on a piece of paper. Take a pen or pencil with you so you can cross out the letters as you find them.

The Type Taster

Opposite: Ilfracombe Type Safari by Karina Monger
Left: Dalston Type Safari by Sarah Hyndman

3. Find the individual letters on the signs that make up your phrase, ideally using a camera with a zoom lens so you can isolate each letter.

4. Have fun and get creative, try a daytime and night-time version for comparison.

5. Combine your photos to spell out your phrase.

Answers
Page 16
Anna's family car is a Ford.

Page 18
Supermarket sweep: *There are six luxury products to be found in each supermarket.* Typefaces: Cooper Black, *Edwardian Script*, Impact, Helvetica, Franklin Gothic Condensed, Candice.

Lawyers typefaces: *Trajan, Stencil, Cinema Italic.*

Ampersand pub typefaces: *Engraver's Old English, Flemish Script, Cooper Black.*

References
1 'There is going to be a celebration at the London Design Festival this year to honour typefaces', Sarah Hyndman interviewed by Justin Webb and Humphrys, Radio 4 *Today*, typetastingnews.com/2013/09/17/radio-4/.
2 'Food Fight' by Steven Heller, 1999, *AIGA* vol 17.
3 'Lessons to be learnt from the Gap logo debacle' by Tom Geoghegan, 2010, *BBC News Magazine*.
4 'The road sign as design classic' by Caroline McClatchey, *BBC News Magazine*.
5 'Why the Same Three Typefaces Are Used In Almost Every Airport' by Alissa Walker, gizmodo.com.
6 'Where in the world am I? The addictive mapping game that is GeoGuessr' by Will Coldwell, *Independent*.

The Ampersand Arms pub name was suggested by Daniel Smithies via Twitter.

The current Type Tasting Tested on Humans surveys and workshops can be found at typetasting.com.

Ol
mes
et. Si p
Fe
gad
Who so my

2
Functional vs evocative

'His Consolation of Philosophy' printed by William
Caxton in 1478, courtesy of St Bride Library & Archives.

1450s 1470s 1500s-1700s 1750s 1780s 1900s

Ae Ae Ae Ae Ae Ae

*Engravers'
Old English*   *Centaur*   *Caslon*   *Baskerville*   *Didot*   *Helvetica*

Blackletter   Humanist   Old Style   Transitional   Modern   Sans Serif

FUNCTIONAL VS EVOCATIVE

Humans are social creatures and the act of communicating with each other, of exchanging experiences and passing on history, has played an important role in our evolutionary survival. The information we share has taught us what is safe and what might be dangerous, helped us to find food and stay healthy, and bonds us together in communities. For millennia this was done through the rich oral tradition of story telling.

Early books were only available to be read by a privileged few because they were time consuming to create. In the middle ages they were meticulously hand copied by monks with beautifully ornate detail. These large, heavy tomes were precious and housed in monasteries and universities. The average person had no access to books so reading was not a skill many needed to learn. Instead, the high street signs of the day featured iconic symbols, some of which we still see in use today; like the striped red and white barber's pole, the pawn broker's three hanging spheres, and the visual interpretations of pub names.

Then everything changed...

The introduction of moveable type to Europe meant that multiple copies of books could now be printed. This was to be a game-changer as books would soon be accessible to the whole population and not just the minority. The first major book to be printed was the Gutenberg Bible (see page 126) which was created by Johannes Gutenberg in Germany in the 1450s. By the 1470s William Caxton had introduced the printing press to England and he also became the first English book retailer[1].

Books were still large and heavy, but within a few decades Aldus Manutius[2] invented italic type which was narrower enabling more words to be printed on a page, and he scaled the size of a book down to make it portable and cheaper to produce. With these developments a much wider audience now had access to knowledge. Literacy rates increased and education was no longer a luxury available only to the wealthy. Ideas could be shared on an unprecedented scale and a knowledge revolution had begun.

Evolution of type

The first printed typefaces were Blackletter type styles which reflected the meticulous handwriting of the scribes. However, these letterforms were intricate to make as metal type and the coarse, absorbent paper of the era was not suited to printing such fine details. Typeface design has always gone hand in hand with developments in printing technology and paper quality. In the 1470s printers turned to simpler type styles which were better suited to the process and materials available to them. They took inspiration from the calligraphy of the Italian humanist writers who created letterforms closer to the Roman inscriptions found on Trajan's column than the heavy, gothic Blackletter scripts.[3] This classification is known as Humanist and the calligraphic influence can be seen in the shape of the letter 'e' (see opposite).

The transformation from Blackletter script to Roman Serifs was a dramatic change of style. But in the five and a half centuries since there has been relatively little change by comparison, even with the arrival of Sans Serifs. By contrast, fashion and transport have changed beyond recognition since the 1400s: from medieval outfits and horse-drawn carriages to what we wear and the transport options of today.

There is an interesting juxtaposition which takes place when type styles from the 15th and 16th century are used on the screens of today's technology. One of the options on a Kindle is *Palatino*[4] which, although designed in the 1940s, is based on the humanist types of the Italian Renaissance and named after 16th century Italian calligrapher Giambattista Palatino. Yet it does not seem out of place used for 21st century technology. Early printed book specialist Tom Nealon[5] talks of the endurability of Nicolas Jenson's Roman type of the 1470s and says this design had "nailed it". He suggests that if you set a book today in Jenson "no one would bat an eye", yet setting it in Blackletter would be like using "runes or Klingon". In the future,

as technology accelerates the pace of change, will typefaces transform beyond recognition or will they continue to reflect these links to history and the printing techniques of the past?

Type is functional

Type functions as a carrier of words. It displays these efficiently so that the reader's eyes can glide seemingly effortlessly across the page as they read. It is sometimes considered that type should be 'invisible' and not intrude on the reading experience. The title of American typographic expert Beatrice Warde's 1930 essay 'The Crystal Goblet'[6] refers to her opinion that type should function like a clear wine glass and purely "carry but not obstruct" the content.

Much research into typefaces explores their readability, focussing on the mechanics of letter shapes and how they function. Testing includes eye tracking and monitoring response times. An example is the research Monotype type foundry has done with MIT[7] into readability of typefaces on car dashboards (see page 125).

There are rules for typography which can be found in many books and blogs on the subject. Over the page is a selection of the most important ones. (See page 134 for examples and explanations of the terminology).

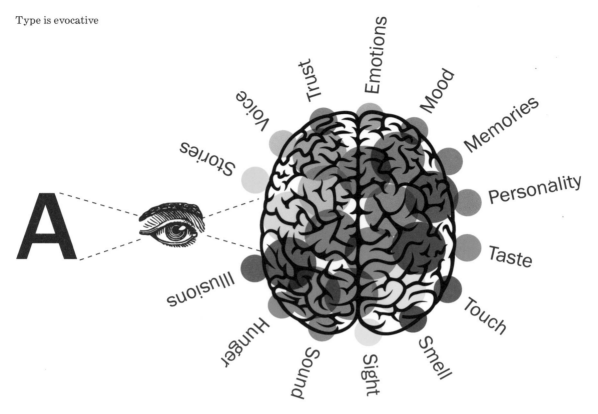

The labels around the brain read: Trust, Emotions, Mood, Memories, Personality, Taste, Touch, Smell, Sight, Sound, Hunger, Illusions, Stories, Voice

1. The size of type should be 8.5–12 points for print, 15–25 pixels for web (depending on the readability of the font).
2. Line length should be between 45–80 characters (including spaces).
3. Pay for good typefaces for professional work, do not use free ones (you get what you pay for).
4. Use centred and justified text sparingly.
5. Use all caps sparingly, it is harder to read and gives the impression that you are SHOUTING.
6. Do not combine too many typefaces.
7. Pale text reversed out of a dark background can be hard to read. Be sensitive to the audience.
8. Do not artificially stretch or compress type.
9. Use a single not a double space at the end of a sentence.
10. Beware of bad kerning or spacing between letters. Check the spacing by looking at the word upside down. (Watch out for accidental swear words created by unfortunate spacing).

However this book is not about the function of fonts or the rules of typography...

Type is evocative

There is more to type than just being an invisible transmitter of words. The different shapes and styles of the typefaces themselves stimulate responses independently of the words they spell out, and before we even read them.

Type triggers our imaginations, evokes our emotions, prompts memories and links to all of our senses. We automatically recognise attributes from the physical world like how loud it looks, whether it is heavy or light, fast or slow or what it would feel like to touch. We have also learned a great deal from our shopping experiences which include knowing whether something is expensive, aimed at children or how it might taste.

It is easy to measure how readable a font is, but it is less straightforward to measure how it makes people feel. As a result, there is less public domain research in this area and much of what we know as designers comes from personal observation and experience.

References
1 'William Caxton', en.wikipedia.org.
2 'Aldus Manutius', typographia.org.
3 'History of typography: Humanist' by John Boardley, 2007, ilovetypography.com.
4 'Kindle Paperwhite' by Stephen Coles, 2012, fontsinuse.com.
5 'Kern Your Enthusiasm 12' by Tom Nealon, 2014, hilobrow.com.
6 'The Crystal Goblet' by Beatrice Warde, 1930, World Publishers. 'The Crystal Goblet' is an essay on typography by Beatrice Warde. The essay was first delivered as a speech, called 'Printing Should Be Invisible', given to the British Typographers' Guild at the St Bride Institute in London on October 7 1930.
7 'Monotype Introduces the Burlingame Typeface Family', press release by Monotype 2014, monotype.com.

The current Type Tasting Tested on Humans surveys and workshops can be found at typetasting.com.

How a typeface functions is practical. It could be compared to building and fine-tuning a car engine for optimum performance. What a typeface evokes is about the experience of being a type consumer and using it. This is like taking a car out for a drive on the wide open road, music playing and appreciating how it makes you feel.

'Typeface' or 'font'?

The TYPEFACE is the design, for example *Helvetica*, this includes the entire family of sizes, styles and weights.

A FONT is the format you experience the typeface in. Traditionally this would have been a set of metal type in a specific size, style and weight: for example 12 point *Helvetica bold*. Today we access typefaces through many more formats and the meaning of the word 'font' has expanded to encompass them. The term now includes the files we access via the font menus on our computers, mobile devices and websites.

I recently explained this to a client who summarised that "a typeface is like my collective family, the Greenes, and the fonts would be the individual Greene family members."

Or you could imagine that the typeface is a film ('Star Wars') and the fonts are the different formats you would watch it in.

The two terms are becoming increasingly interchangeable and I think conversations about type should not be overshadowed by terminology anxiety.

Typefaces	*Helvetica*	Greene family	'Star Wars'

| Fonts | Helvetica thin, 8 pt
Helvetica thin italic, 8 pt
Helvetica light cond., 8 pt
Helvetica light cond. italic, 8 pt
Helvetica, 8 pt
Helvetica italic, 8 pt
Helvetica heavy, 8 pt
Helvetica heavy italic, 8 pt
Helvetica heavy ext.,
Helvetica heavy ext. | | |

3

How do fonts influence you?

Audience at Sarah Hyndman's talk for the London Design Festival at the V&A, 2014. Photo by Martin Naidu.

HOW DO FONTS INFLUENCE YOU?

Before reading this chapter take the challenge in this short film: **typetasting.com/movie.html** (*Reading on might give the game away*).[1]

Is type a conspiracy? Does it coerce you with secret messages hidden from view? No, far from it. Type appears right in front of your eyes and is clear for you to see. It is your choice not to pay attention to it consciously and to focus on reading what the words actually say. The type itself is still transmitting plenty of information, it is just communicating it directly to your subconscious.

Font Goggles

Typefaces/fonts prime you with a great deal of information and set the scene for the words you are about to read. They give words a back story, a personality, clue you in to whether or not you can trust them, whether they will be serious or light hearted, academic or childish. Generally, well-set type is designed so that you 'look past' the typeface and focus on the words themselves—unless of course the font does not match, like somebody with a bad haircut or a miscast actor in a film (page 56).

At any time you can choose to pay attention and look at the fonts themselves. Use the red/blue Font Goggles included with this book to reveal what some of them could be communicating directly to your subconscious brain in the red/blue images throughout this chapter.

(a) Cover (or close) one eye so that you are looking through the blue lens. Through this lens you will simply read what the words spell out.

(b) Now look through the red lens and join me in 'type wonderland' where you will see what the fonts themselves might be telling you.[2]

*allegedly

Sleight of hand

Neuroscientist Dr David Lewis describes type as being "hidden in plain sight"[3] and explains that it transmits information "supraliminally" which means it is within the threshold of awareness. This is the opposite of subliminal, which takes place outside your awareness; for example it might happen too quickly for you to register it. You can choose whether to notice supraliminal messages, but you are not aware of subliminal messages.

	Supraliminal	Supraliminal	Supraliminal	Su
'E	**BUY ME**	**BUY ME**	**BUY ME**	B
	⏱ 0:020	⏱ 0:030	⏱ 0:040	⏱ 0
l	Subliminal	Subliminal	Subliminal	S
		BUY ME		
	⏱ 0:020	⏱ 0:030	⏱ 0:040	⏱ 0

Examples of subliminal messages are the 'blipverts' which featured in the 'Max Headroom' sci-fi film in the 1980s. These were television adverts shown so quickly that they influenced viewers subliminally without them realising. At the time these prompted concern that advertisers were really using these to brainwash customers.

Examples of supraliminal communicators are the score or soundtrack to a film, the smell of food, and typefaces, all of which we will look at in more detail in this chapter.

In his article 'The Art of Honest Deception' author Vincent H. Gaddis explains that a magician's skill is not that he can perform tricks too quickly for the eye to see, his skill is in cleverly misdirecting the attention of the audience during the performance. He says that magic tricks are successful because they are "nine-tenths simple distraction".[4] Printed words are like magicians, they distract you from paying attention to the fonts and instead you concentrate on reading what they say.

Typefaces and magic tricks both take place right in front of our eyes but somehow they can seem invisible. Lewis describes this as "perceptual blindness", explaining that we "don't perceive what we don't attend to".[5] Professor Daniel J. Simons

dur du **dur** du **dur** du

calls it "inattentional blindness" for the same reason. Simons demonstrates this well in 'The Monkey Business Illusion'. This is the challenge from the short film at the beginning of this chapter.[6]

Wood for the trees

One of the things I have learnt from my experiences as a graphic designer is to proofread large type in titles and headlines carefully because this is where spelling mistakes can go unnoticed. It is easy to get so focussed on the small details of a design project that we can forget to take a step back and only spot the spelling mistake (with that heart-sinking feeling) once the project is finished and printed. This is a classic example of 'not seeing the wood for the trees'.

I once arranged to meet a friend in Liverpool Street Station under the "really big departures board". After a while she rang me to say she could not find it because there were too many signs. When I found her I said "look up" because she was standing right underneath it but she had

been so busy looking at all the small signs she had not noticed the huge one that ran the full width of the station.

Under the influence

Type sets the tone and gives you clues about what you are about to read. The headlines and titles often feature display typefaces that have larger than life characteristics. This works much like the music in a film, which sets the scene for what you are about to watch. The soundtrack tells you whether you can relax, whether to feel sad, or if you should start to feel anxious and get ready to close your eyes before the action actually happens.

It is the iconic music in 'Jaws' that creates the tension and primes you to be teetering right on the edge of your seat and ready to jump long before the shark actually appears.

In 'Alien' the noise gets increasingly frenetic, building up to the moment when the creature suddenly bursts out of John Hurt's chest.

Helvetica / Flemish Script

Cooper Black

VAG Rounded AG

In the film 'The Ring' it is the unanswered phone that makes the scene so creepy as you watch the figure climb out of the well on the television screen. I recently watched this with the sound turned off and not only was it no longer scary but it became almost comical.

Shops and supermarkets are aware that many factors like type, design, music and what we smell can influence how we shop—but without us being aware of this consciously.[7,8] In an article on subliminal selling, Dr David Lewis refers to a study which found that if there was classic rock playing in a shop, 'baby boomers' were more likely to make purchases. Yet when they were asked about it afterwards two-thirds did not even remember what music had been playing.

In another study C. S. Gulas and C. D. Schewe[9] show that wine buyers will purchase more expensive wine when classical music is playing in a shop. Napa based graphic designer David Schuemann specialises in designing wine labels[10] and says "we always make a wine look about $10 more expensive than it is".

Arial black

Didot

Flemish Script

The smell of freshly baked bread or roast chicken wafting through a food shop can have you heading for the bakery aisle or picking up the ingredients for a roast dinner, even if you had no desire to eat either before walking into the shop. I find this also happens to me when I smell fresh coffee or see the font used by my favourite coffee shop.

What am I telling you?

Agincourt

What am I telling you?

Didot

What am I telling you?

Helvetica

What are these fonts telling you?
Using a pale blue felt tip, write your
answers over the top of each typeface.

Next time you are out shopping and you find
yourself with items in your basket that you had not
planned to purchase, stop and become aware of
all the stimuli around you. Are there external
factors influencing your purchasing choices?

Sponsored fonts

When I scroll down my font menu I see some
typefaces that I associate with brands. Opinion
is divided on whether a company's typeface being
in the public domain for everybody to use dilutes
its brand image, or whether its increased presence
is a clever form of advertising for a strong brand.

When I see *Cooper Black*[11] I think of the EasyJet
logo. The typeface looks to me like comfortable
pillow-like clouds and I find I can easily start
daydreaming about holidays.

Also in the list is *VAG Rounded* which was
designed for Volkswagen AG in 1979. Making it
available to the company worldwide was a problem
at the time. To get around this the font was put into
the public domain and was soon included in most

free font packages[12]. Although it is no longer
their corporate typeface, the link will always be
preserved in the name.

I think there is an opening for a big brand to
commission a hand-written style typeface family
as an alternative to *Comic Sans* which could be
bundled for free with standard operating system
software. Since a large proportion of the audience
would be schools and children I would hope it is
a brand promoting positive and healthy values, or
that encourages curiosity, and not one advertising
fast food.

Sinaloa

Wainwright

Madame

References

1 'Monkeying around with the gorillas in our midst: Familiarity with an inattentional-blindness task does not improve the detection of unexpected events' by Professor Daniel J. Simons, 2010, i-Perception.
www.youtube.com/watch?v=IGQmdoK_ZfY.
2 'Red pill and blue pill', en.wikipedia.org.
"The red pill and its opposite, the blue pill, are popular culture symbols representing the choice between embracing the sometimes painful truth of reality (red pill) and the blissful ignorance of illusion (blue pill)."
3 *The Brain Sell: When Science Meets Shopping* by David Lewis.
4 'The Art of Honest Deception', by Vincent H. Gaddis, strangemag.com.
5 'Subliminal Selling' by Dr David Lewis, themindlab.co.uk.
6 Ibid Professor Daniel J. Simons.
7 (ref Subliminal Selling by Dr David Lewis on the themindlab.co.uk.
8 'Using background music to affect the behaviour of supermarket shoppers' by Milliman, R. E. 1982, *Journal of Marketing*, 46 (3), 86-91.).
9 Gulas, C. S. & Schewe, C.D. (1994). Atmospheric segmentation: Managing Store Image With Background Music, Enhancing Knowledge Development in Marketing, Ravi Achrol & Andrew Mitchell (Eds.), Chicago IL: American Marketing Association, 325-330.
10 'Drinking With Your Eyes: How Wine Labels Trick Us Into Buying' by Michaeleen Doucleff, 2013, kqed.org.
11 'Cooper Black' by Oswald Bruce Cooper in 1921.
12 'VAG Rounded' by Gerry Barney et al.,wikipedia.org.

The current Type Tasting Tested on Humans surveys and workshops can be found at typetasting.com.

hello **hello** hello

hello **hello** **hello**

hello hello **hello**

hello hello **hello**

hello *hello* hello

hello **hello** hello

hello *hello* hello

hello hello hello

4

Type Karaoke

Helvetica's vocal range

Arkeo

Black Boton

Franklin Gothic

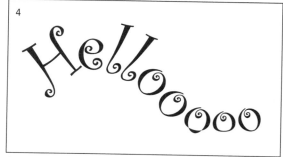

Curlz

TYPE KARAOKE

Play the game of Type Karaoke above by simply saying what you see. Try it out on friends, family or play it with a group of children.

Type can function as a human voice transmitter and convey the tones and qualities of your voice visually. We each have a unique voice that communicates a great deal about us like our gender and age. It charts where we come from, who we know and where we have lived along the way. Could your voice look like the traditionally British and approachable *Gill Sans*, or the more intellectual *Caslon*?

Graphic designer Ellen Lupton describes typography as "what language looks like".[1] If you imagine that your voice is the typeface, then your vocal range is created by the sizes, styles and weights of fonts within that typeface family and how they are arranged on the page. Even a simple text message can be written expressively from speaking very s l o w l y to SHOUTING. Think how you feel when you receive a text or an email written in all upper case letters?

Clive Lewis and Peter Walker see the printed word as a visual code for speech which creates a permanent record of both (a) how the words sound when spoken and (b) what they mean.[2]

In her famous 1930 essay[3] Beatrice Warde compares typeface legibility to the human voice and suggests that if three pages are set in *Fournier*, *Caslon* and *Plantin* typefaces it would be like "three different people delivering the same discourse—each with impeccable pronunciation and clarity, yet each through the medium of a different personality."

Visual onomatopoeia

We all understand instinctively that type mirrors qualities from the physical world and interpretations are consistently similar from one person to the next. A bold font with more ink coverage on the paper looks loud, and if it is large enough to fill the field of vision then it appears so close it comes across as extremely loud. A small word looks a long way away and sounds distant and quiet. The arrangements of

Helvetica Neue ultra light compressed

Flemish Script

Riptide

Modified *Impact*

the letters on the page are easily read, like musical inflection, and you will match your tone of voice to this as you read.

Balega

Type designer Jürgen Weltin says of his 2003 typeface *Balega*,[4] that with its contrasting curves and sharp edges it would ring with the "fat sound of a Jimi Hendrix guitar."

On page 41 there are some of the descriptions from an online survey, 'What would typefaces sound like if they were music?'

Gill Sans

I always imagine that *Gill Sans* would speak with a 'BBC English' accent. It would pronounce words and use grammar correctly but have a friendly and relaxed tone, a few notches down from the formality of the Queen's English. It is the typeface used for the BBC logo which was designed in the late 1920s and is reminiscent of 1930s England.

Type and Sound workshop

So far in this chapter we have explored what existing fonts would sound like. In one Type Tasting Type and Sound workshop we take sound as a starting point and go through the process of using it to inspire new letterforms. The final alphabets demonstrate how letterforms can convey the nuances of different sounds.

In this exercise participants are played three different sounds in turn. These are heavy metal music, waves on a beach and a screaming woman from a horror film. As they listen they fill a sheet of paper with scribbles and marks inspired by each sound using appropriate materials.

Once the three sheets have been filled with marks the participants search for letterforms in each and cut them out. At the end they have created three distinct alphabets, each of which reflects the qualities of the sounds that inspired it.

See Lydia CS's sound project over the page.

Type and Sound workshop
Sketches and sound alphabets (A to E) by Lydia CS

Heavy metal music:

Waves on a beach:

Screaming woman:

Type Tasting online survey 'What would typefaces sound like if they were music?'

sound

Robot, retro, techno, crisp, digital, discordant, edgy, futuristic, clipped, green, bright, icy, juttery, solid, snappy, firm, trebly, edgy, resonant, tinny, atonal, loud, cacophonous, cutting, clipped, edgy, deep, robot, classic, booming, quick, repetitive, auto-tuned, soulful, techno, technical, modern, digitised, retro, underground, boxy, sci-fi, electronic, techno, ugly, thematic, technical, beat-box, electric, '80s, funky, different, space age, bleak, haunting, quirky, artificial, techno-beat, industrial, serious, oppressive.
It makes me feel anxious.
(*Cinema*)

sound

Sophisticated, mellifluous, melodious, relaxing, classic, mellow, smooth, deep, mature, warm, rounded, round, soft, smooth, heavy, comfy, curved, deep, bass, bassy, melodious, loud, low, blue, melodic, slow, fluid, bouncy, gentle, retro, mature, sure, sophisticated, soul, classic, full, soulful, classy, psychedelic, old, complex, austere, jazzy, traditional, ice cream, dated, modern, summery, sexy, romantic, relaxing, happy, pleasing, mellow, calm, mellow, fun, chilled, serene, immersing.
It makes me feel happy and calm.
(*Bodoni Poster italic*)

sound

Jarring, sharp, energetic, harsh, tinny, edgy, dramatic, piercing, uncomfortable, modern, cool, cold, bright, vibrant, scratchy, spiky, prickly, jagged, angular, tinny, high-pitched, jangly, percussive, loud, pitchy, shrill, discordant, piercing, high, stuck, fast, quick, energetic, staccato, brief, erratic, jerky, jittery, strict, punk, funky, modern, quirky, electronic, futuristic, urban, repetitive, rave, ear-piercing, different, noisy, synthesised, dramatic, young, angst, agitating, exciting, uncomfortable, aggressive.
It makes me feel anxious.
(*Modified Klute*)

sound

Safe, young, playful, soft, boring, balanced, childish, calming, straightforward, sonorous, fresh, cool, vibrant, heavy, rounded, soft, round, wooden, solid, smooth, tympanic, full, sonorous, resonant, even, smooth, clear, ringing, melodic, loud, booming, ambling, fluid, bouncy, breezy, mundane, simple, standard, perfect, clean, classy, clear, neat, friendly, basic, easy, simple, child-like, clichéd, bold, boring, clear, safe, comforting, relaxed, upbeat, pleasant, happy, confident, sad, calming, playful, gentle.
It makes me feel happy and calm.
(*VAG Rounded*)

References
1 *Thinking with Type* by Ellen Lupton, 2010, Princeton Architectural Press.
2 'Typographic influences on reading' by Clive Lewis and Peter Walker, 1989, British *Journal of Psychology*.
3 'The Crystal Goblet' by Beatrice Warde, 1930, World Publishers.
4 'Balega' by Jürgen Weltin, 2003, membership.monotype.com.
The current Type Tasting Tested on Humans surveys and workshops can be found at typetasting.com.

(a)

(b)

(c)

(f)

(g)

(h)

5

Fonts turn words into stories

(d)

(e)

Book genres by type
(a) *Slipstream,* (b) *Wainwright,* (c) *Arnold Boecklin,* (d) *Engraver's Old English,* (e) *Flemish Script,* (f) *Bludgeon,*
(g) *Retro Bold,* (h) *Comic Sans,* (i) *Data 70,* (j) *Stencil.*

(i)

(j)

A font transforms the meaning of a word

FONTS TURN WORDS INTO STORIES

"Come with me and you'll be in a world of your imagination." Willy Wonka[1].

Typography is storytelling. Typefaces set the scene and clue you in to what the words will reveal independently of what they actually say. This is something referred to by psychologists Clive Lewis and Peter Walker as "typographic allusion".[2] By doing this, fonts give words a back story and a personality, they establish meaning and sometimes they subvert the meaning of the words. Your interpretation of a word can be brought to life by the typeface it is set in.

There is a coffee shop I go to which has one wall completely lined with books with only the spines on view. The book jackets have been reduced down to typography and colour with all the different styles giving tantalising glimpses of the stories to be found inside the books. Often it is the typeface that draws my eye to a particular book and makes it look so much more interesting than the one sitting next to it.

Responses, associations or knowledge?

1. Instinctive responses
You react instinctively to some typefaces and respond purely to their shape. These responses are hardwired into your DNA for your survival and protection. For example you intuitively know that round shapes are safe and friendly whilst jagged shapes are dangerous or aggressive (see page 69).

2. Learned associations
You have a library of associations in your brain which you have been collecting all your life. This happens every time you see a typeface from the context in which you see it used. Some of these can be almost universally recognised, others are specific to you and your own unique experiences.

These associations can remain constant, unaltered over time—or they can change, with the flick of an event that adds to their history and creates a completely new set of associations. For example, Blackletter was used for the first books printed in Germany in the 1400s. These styles were based on the handwriting of monks and have associations with timeless wisdom and precious books like The Bible. However, when Hitler declared Blackletter to be the official type style of the Nazi Party, this ancient and romantic type style acquired a new and darker set of associations that have become permanently entwined into its history.

Tobias Frere-Jones designed the *Gotham* typeface family for 'GQ' magazine. It is based on the mid-twentieth century geometric type found on vernacular signage in New York.[3] When *Gotham* was used to spell out 'hope' and 'change' in Obama's 2008 presidential campaign it became the typeface of 'inspiration and optimism' and is now so widely used that it has joined the ranks of the celebrity typefaces.

"No typefaces are immune to history" Neville Brody.[4]

Since we gather these learned associations throughout our lives, then older generations could have a much broader frame of reference for type since they have spent "many more years becoming acclimatised to the links between fonts, products and experiences" according to retirement sector journalist Alex Finkenrath. Just take a look at other areas of popular culture, like music, where parents of every generation have uttered the phrase, "I had the original version of that song" to a child who thinks they are listening to something brand new.

3. Learned knowledge
This is the domain of the expert who, like an art critic or a wine connoisseur, has acquired a great deal of knowledge of the subject. The expert generally interacts with type as a professional designer and not just as a consumer, which can mean that they often perceive a typeface to have much more complex qualities (see page 81).

A font is in the eye of the beholder

As graphic designers, we take advantage of these links and associations. We use these visual codes to enable us to communicate messages effectively and to create layers of meaning. By doing this we also reinforce and strengthen this code of references through repetition.

Designers combine typefaces with words using different levels of complexity:

1. The font matches the words
The advantage of using a type style which mirrors what the words say is that the words can be understood easily from a quick glance. There may be occasions where this is important.

WESTERN

Wainwright

Romance

Edwardian Script

2. The font adds extra meaning to the words
The typeface works a little harder and conveys

extra information that adds extra meaning to the words. Here the western is now set in Mexico and the romance is an army adventure story.

Mesquite

Stencil

3. The font alters the meaning of the words
Now the western is now set in the sci-fi world of outer space and the romance is clearly not destined for a happy ending.

WESTERN

Futura

Bludgeon

Moving away from clichés

The 'Read Me' books on pages 42–43 have covers that epitomise particular genres. Which cover fits each of these categories: 1960s sci-fi, vampire story, comedy, action thriller, romance in Paris, army adventure, classic romance, rebel against society, western, horror (answers on page 53).

Moving away from clichés enables the type to create intrigue and to become more complex by adding layers of meaning. The typeface can allude to additional ideas and the designer now relies on the reader's knowledge of these references to recognise and understand the combined meanings. The word treatments at the top of page 44 show how the meanings of the words have been transformed to suggest more complex stories.

Do you believe the type?

As designers we can use type to imply things that we would not be able to say in words, or which might be untrue if shown as a photograph. For example if a beef burger is mass produced in a factory it would be a lie to say 'hand made' on the packaging. It would also be untrue to show an image of somebody making it by hand. However, we can use a typeface that implies the product is hand made and the consumer may assume it is an

(a)
Comedy

(b)
Romantic comedy

(c)
ANY MOVIE

accurate description of the product. This is a widely used advertising technique. Do you think you have ever fallen for this?

BURGER

BURGER

Compare the two typefaces above; which product do you assume is hand made? Which would you pay more for? You will likely find yourself enjoying the taste of the second burger more because you expect to, even if they are both the same burger (see page 115).

Semiotics and film posters

There are continuing discussions about whether type should simply be an unseen transmitter of words; it was mentioned earlier that Beatrice Warde taught that type should be 'invisible' (page 25).[5] I think well-designed type can appear transparent and not intrude on the reading experience, but that it does not remain neutral.

Semiotics[6], which became popular in the 1960s, is the study of signs and meanings. According to its principles, an object becomes inextricably linked with ideas or associations you make from the context in which you encounter it. Not only does the object lose its neutrality, it also goes on to become a transmitter of the additional meanings. Both the object and the meaning combine to become a 'sign'. For example a red rose is linked to the idea of romance and, once you have learned this, it is hard to think of one without the other.

Writer Yves Peters[7] researches the typography of film posters and shows that some typefaces have come to signify particular film genres because they have been used so repetitively that they have created a graphic code (see above). You cannot see a particular typeface without the genre coming to mind.

(a) Comedy titles are generally in bold Sans Serif typefaces like *Gill Sans ultra bold*.

(b) Romantic comedies generally use Modern/Didone typefaces such as *Didot*.

(c) The typeface *Trajan* was first used for 'epic inspirational films', but it has now appeared so frequently across all genres that it has become the ubiquitous typeface of the movies. It was even adopted by the Oscars themselves in 2006.

In The
Blackmoor

Beginning
Goudy Text

Type
Agincourt

emulated the
Luthersche Fraktur

handwriting
Engravers' Old English

of scribes
Fette Gotisch

Humanist
Eg *Centaur*

circa 1470 de

Calligraphic influence
sloping crossbar on 'e'
low thick/thin contrast
sloped stress

Italic
Eg *Garamond italic*

circa 1500 *de*

Old Style
Eg *Caslon*

circa 1500 de

Horizontal crossbar on 'e'
greater thick/thin contrast
more upright stress

Transitional
Eg *Baskerville*

circa 1700 de

More refined serifs
greater thick/thin contrast
upright stress

Modern
Eg *Didot*

circa 1780 de

Abrupt (unbracketed) serifs
extreme thick/thin contrast
upright stress

Slab
Eg *Egyptian 710*

circa 1800 de

Bold 'slab' shaped serifs

In the beginning

The first printed typefaces were created in the 1450s. These were based on the detailed writing of the monks and scribes who hand copied books before the advent of print. Our modern eye can find these styles overly ornate and difficult to read in quantity, but if you agree with type designer Zuzanna Licko's premise that you "read best what you read the most"[8] then Blackletter could be thought of as the *Helvetica* of its day.

Blackletter has absorbed many associations in its long history from the different contexts in which you have seen it used. These include the romance of Arthurian legends, the rebellion of heavy metal music, the links to tradition through newspaper mastheads, the darkness of vampire films and the authenticity of German beer labels.

Traditional and knowledgeable

Serif typefaces date back over five centuries to the first decades of printing in Europe and they have become steeped in associations of history, knowledge and tradition. Many books, especially older books, are set in Roman Serif styles, as are traditional newspapers. As a result we have come to associate these with conveying serious and credible information.

Anna Alternates

Anna Extended

DECO

CELEBRATED

Huxley Vertical

LUXURY

Sinaloa

GLAMOUR

Copasetic

AND THE

Matra

MACHINE AGE

Plaza Swash

Young Baroque

RICH

Engravers MT

ENGRAVED

Caslon Titling

AND

Chevalier

Calligraphic

Flemish Script

Nostalgic luxury

Art Deco became popular from the 1920s and 1930s. It stood for modernity and progress and offered an escape from traditional conventions.[9] Many cinemas and music halls were built in England in this era and both the architecture and signage can still be seen. These type styles are popular on bar signs for their associations with the decadence of speakeasies in the prohibition era.

Money, money, money

The typefaces above are all about money and are inspired by the style of engraved typography found on bank notes, deeds and bearer bonds. Formal scripts similar to *Young Baroque* are based on the skilled letterforms of 18th century master calligraphers, who used a quill or metal nib of a pen. The Roman style letters like *Chevalier* have fine lines, details and sharp serifs typical of engraved styles.

The intricate designs on bank notes are engraved by hand onto metal plates by engravers like Tony Maidment. This is a highly-skilled craft and the work by each engraver is individual like handwriting or a fingerprint. The nuances of lines and dots, unique to the style of each engraver, are one of the main weapons against counterfeiting.[10]

F

Didot Headline

IS FOR

Bodoni

fashion

Didot

type for a

Industria

REVO-
LUTION

Retro Bold

BREAKS FREE FROM

Pritchard

*East Bloc
Phosphor*

THE
GRID

Fashion fonts

Typefaces with extremely contrasting thick and thin elements are classified as Moderns or Didones. These were developed in the late 1700s by Firmin Didot in France and Giambattista Bodoni in Italy, who were famous rivals. Improvements in paper quality and printing technology enabled them to print letters with extremely fine details and crisp, sharp edges.

These have been used widely on fashion magazines like 'Vogue' and 'Harper's Bazaar', dating back to the 1920s and as a result we now think of them as epitomising femininity, style and fashion.[11, 12]

Revolutionary type

Avant Garde art movements of the late 19th and early 20th centuries like Constructivism, De Stijl, Futurism and Dada, have dynamic visual styles which treat type as imagery, allowing it to break free of the structured grid.

These are the movements of revolution and change; they pushed boundaries and embraced dynamic progress. They celebrated noise, momentum and energy.

Famous Avant Garde designers who worked with type include El Lissitzky, Rodchenko and Filippo Tommaso Marinetti.

RULE
Gill Sans Shadow

Brittania
Johnston

from Baskerville
Baskerville

& Caslon to the
Caslon italic '&', Caslon

GREAT
Festival Titling

humanist
Gill Sans heavy

sans serifs
Johnston bold

Appleton

Victorian

Algerian

Friz Quadrata

AdHoc

Brody

Flash

Made in Britain

This collection of typefaces is a celebration of Britishness. *Gill Sans* is a Humanist Sans Serif with a hand-drawn feel to its shapes. It was designed by the artist and type designer Eric Gill. Gill was a student of Edward Johnston, creator of *Johnston* for the London Underground. (In my opinion *Johnston* is the unofficial typeface of London.) *Baskerville* and *Caslon* represent the rich British history of type design which dates back to the 1600s, with typefaces such as these exported around the world. *Caslon* was used for the Declaration of Independence. *Festival Titling* was the typeface created for the 1951 Festival of Britain and it still evokes 1950s nostalgia.

Writing on the wall

Painted lettering on signs became popular in England in the 18th century with the increase in literacy due to printed books and newspapers becoming more widely available.[13] Sign writers were the original 'brand designers', as they created the signage on the front of shops and businesses. There is a current resurgence of interest in the craft of sign writing with many more signs being traditionally hand painted. They often include signature details, like a flourish on the crossbar of the 'A', and you can learn to recognise which craftsman's work it is.

Blackoak

Egyptian Slate

Wainwright

Falstaff

Enge Holzschrift

Magnifico Daytime

Broadcast Titling

Aesthetique

Thunderbird

Madame

Wood Relief

Victorian

Saraband Initials

Going large

The Industrial Revolution in the late 18th century enabled products to be manufactured in excess of demand. The advertising industry was born as manufacturers now needed to promote and sell products. Posters and advertisements had to stand out in crowded environments, on the sides of moving trains or viewed at angles and so bigger and bolder display typefaces were created.

Fat Face typefaces, similar to *Falstaff*, are bloated versions of Modern/Didone styles (see page 49). Then serifs were stretched and made chunkier, creating Slab Serif typefaces similar to *Egyptian Slate*. Later, condensed Sans Serifs and 3D layered type were added into the mix.

Ornamental type

In the 19th century the Victorians embraced ornamentation and decorated most of the objects in their environment. This included fashion, furniture, architecture and also typeface design. Sign writers added flourishes and textures like gold leaf, and printers carved increasingly ornate letters creating three dimensional illusions and which often featured motifs of everyday life and of nature. Some of the most highly ornamented were created by Louis John Pouchée[14] and can be viewed in the St Bride Library in London.

OUT IN
Eurostile Extended 2

SPACE
Sonic XBd

TYPE IS
Futura light

GEOMETRIC
Dex Gothic

sometimes
petro
Amelia

AND APPEARS
Space

BUILT BY
Flatiron

MACHINE
Computer

Modernism
Helvetica Neue medium

Change
Univers black

&
Neue Haas Grotesk black

Neutrality
Univers light

Function
Neue Haas Grotesk light

NOT
Neue Haas Grotesk bold

Ornamentation
Helvetica Neue italic

Intergalactic communication

Many sci-fi typefaces are based on geometric shapes. These look mechanically constructed, giving the impression they were created in a future 'machine age'. They incorporate a graphic language which can imply an underlying theme: if the type is from an optimistic future utopia, a dark dystopia, or a retro version of the future like typeface *Amelia*, which looks like it's been beamed directly from the 1970s. *Eurostile* and the geometric *Futura* have both appeared in so many sci-fi films that they have become the 'corporate fonts' of sci-fi.

Style follows function

In the first half of the 20th century graphic design generally looked busy and cluttered. Serif style typefaces were combined with images and ornamentation that often filled all of the space on the page. With the arrival of Modernism in the 1950s design was simplified, and used Sans Serif typefaces arranged on a grid structure with lots of white space. Unnecessary details were removed and style was led by function. Sans Serif typefaces were chosen for their neutrality, because they were not steeped in the associations of history. The ubiquitous *Helvetica* (originally *Neue Haas Grotesk*) came out of this era and has since reached celebrity status, even starring in its own film.

Quiz: What type of pub is each of these?
(See page 133 to compare your answers to the Type Tasting survey responses).

Answers
(a) Action thriller, (b) western, (c) romance in Paris, (d) vampire story, (e) classic romance, (f) horror, (g) rebel against society, (h) comedy, (i) 1960s sci-fi, (j) army adventure.

References
1 *Willy Wonka and the Chocolate Factory*, by Leslie Bricusse & Anthony Newley, 1971.
2 'Typographic influences on reading study' by Clive Lewis and Peter Walker, 1989, *British Journal of Psychology*.
3 'The Origin of Gotham' by Hoefler & Co., typography.com.
4 'Unquiet Film Series: Times New Roman' by *The Times* and *The Sunday Times*, foreverunquiet.co.uk.
5 'The Crystal Goblet' by Beatrice Warde 1930, World Publishers.
6 'Semiotics for Beginners' by Daniel Chandler, visual-memory.co.uk.
7 'Trajan in movie posters: the rise and fall of the Roman Empire' by Yves Peters, 2011, Beyond Tellerrand Conference.
8 'Interview with Zuzana Licko' by Rudy VanderLans, *Emigre*.
9 'Art Deco around the World', V&A.
10 'Feature: The secret art of the engraver' by Mark Sinclair, *Creative Review*.
11 'Through thick and thin: fashion and type' by Abbott Miller, *Eye Magazine*.
12 'A Brief History of Type Part Four: Modern (Didone)' by John Boardley, ilovetypography.com.
13 'The English Signwriting Tradition' by Richard Gregory, signpainting.co.uk.
14 'Pouchee's lost alphabets' by Mike Daines, *Eye*.

The current Type Tasting Tested on Humans surveys and workshops can be found at typetasting.com.

1

PATRICK BATEMAN

212.555.6342
PIERCE & PIERCE

WHAT JOB DO I DO?

- -

2

Patrick Bateman

212.555.6342
Pierce & Pierce

What job do I do?

- -

3

Patrick Bateman

212.555.6342
Pierce & Pierce

What job do I do?

- -

4

Patrick Bateman

212.555.6342
Pierce & Pierce

What job do I do?

- -

5

Patrick Bateman

212.555.6342
Pierce & Pierce

What job do I do?

- -

6

Patrick Bateman

212.555.6342
Pierce & Pierce

What job do I do?

- -

7

Patrick Bateman

212.555.6342
Pierce & Pierce

What job do I do?

- -

8

Patrick Bateman

212.555.6342
Pierce & Pierce

What job do I do?

- -

6

Don't believe the type

Play the 'What job do I do?' business card game on the left.
Turn to page 84 to compare your answers to the Type Tasting survey responses.
1: *Trajan*, 2: *Monotype Corsiva*, 3: *Cocon*, 4: *Clarendon*, 5: *Bodoni Poster*, 6: *Didot*, 7: *Comic Sans*, 8: *Cinema italic*

rat
tortoise
heavy
light
strong
light
heavy

fast
slow
elephant
weak
gazelle
weak
elephant

fast
gazelle
tortoise
slow
strong
rat

Quiz: Speed Test

DON'T BELIEVE THE TYPE

You have an intuitive sense of when type fits the situation and when it doesn't. When the type is appropriate to the content it enhances the reading experience, which becomes seemingly effortless as a result. If you watch a film with well-cast actors you are able to sit back, suspend disbelief and enjoy it. If they are poorly cast then the film will not ring true and this can spoil even a great story. This does not mean that the actors go unseen, it means that they complement the scenario. In the same way, well-designed type is not invisible, it works in harmony with the content.

Processing fluency

When you see something written in an unfamiliar typeface your reading experience is interrupted because you need to pay attention to deciphering the letters. This means that you read more slowly and you are likely to become aware of the reading process. By contrast, when you read a familiar type style your eyes are able to "skim effortlessly across the text" and, according to Dr David Lewis, this earns your trust.[1, 2] He calls this 'processing fluency'

as it describes the ease with which you recognise and comprehend what the words say. He goes on to explain that the more easily a customer can process and understand a sales message, the more likely they are to purchase an item. Processing fluency applies not only to the readability of the typeface itself, but also to the design, layout and language. If a highly readable typeface is poorly typeset and difficult to read it will still slow the reader down.

However, this is not proposing that 'one font fits all', as different typefaces will suit different scenarios. The ease with which you read a typeface is a combination of it being both familiar and fitting the context.

Quiz: Speed Test

Set a timer or a stopwatch for 30 seconds. Start the timer and circle all the words at the top of this page where the font DOES NOT match the word. That is, where the meaning of the word seems opposite to the style of the typeface. For example, if the word 'fast' is in a typeface that looks heavy and slow. How many did you find? The answers are on page 63.

The Type Taster

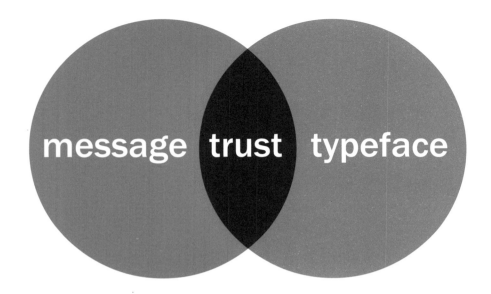

message trust typeface

This speed test quiz is inspired by a study called 'Typographic influences on reading' by Clive Lewis and Peter Walker[3] in which participants were shown a selection of words like 'elephant' and 'fast' typeset either in chunky *Cooper Black,* or the light and speedy looking *Palatino italic*. These are the two typefaces used in the Speed Test quiz. The meaning of some words were mirrored by the shape of the typefaces and, as in the quiz, some appeared to be the opposite. They were given specific words to look out for and asked to press a button as soon as they saw them.

It was found that participants were able to identify the words much faster when they matched the fonts, and that their reaction times were considerably slower when they did not match. They were able to demonstrate that we read much faster when the typeface matches the content.

Influential types

In the world of business some typefaces are more appropriate for certain professions than others, and you are more likely to trust a business card in an appropriate style. On page 18 you selected the lawyer you would hire which was either (a), (b) or (c). Would you have made a different choice if you had wanted a quick and discount lawyer for something routine and unimportant?

LAWYER   **LAWYER**   *Lawyer*

(a)   (b)   (c)

For lawyers (d) to (f) below the choice is less clear cut because all three look appropriate for the legal profession. You now need to make your decision based on personal preference and research.

LAWYER   *Lawyer*   LAWYER

(d)   (e)   (f)

Many professions have recognisable typeface conventions—especially established industries where the preference is likely to be for traditional, conservative and relatively neutral faces that suggest history. Often these have links to Roman inscriptions, engravings or ancient manuscripts that give the impression of longevity and wisdom.

The News

ANCIENT CAT FOUND ON MARS

Lorem ipsum dolor sit amet, at nam tempor deterruisset, sonet facete verear eu mei, cum ad dicam ubique discere. Animal definitiones usu cu, dicat probatus at eum. Ex nominavi aliquando pri, tation altera lobortis ut sit. Te mei possit praesent, no timeam commune intellegat his, reque moderatius an mei. At graece animal mea. Sententiae theophrastus usu an, per omnium assentior eu. Mei errem munere vituperata id. Cum ne maiorum alienum, duo tation laboramus in. Soluta prompta vel in, ad his prima error. Id nec minimum omnesque apparent, te alii tollit decore mei, ignota evertitur rationibus mea ex. Mea habeo bonorum et. Ea quas illud prodesset vix, est ad eruditi fuisset, est at theophrastus definitiones. Habeo iisque veritus mea et. Est cu hendrerit

Mei errem munere vituperata id. Cum ne maiorum alienum, duo tation laboramus in. Soluta prompta vel in, ad his prima error. Id nec minimum definitiones. Habeo hendrerit interpret mediocritatem in. E eros porro at pri, s pro te. Mea habe prodesset vix, es theophrastus defin mea et. Est cu hen referrentur medioc iracundia, eros p comprehensam pr Sententiae theoph assentior eu. Mel

Mea habeo bonoru vix, est ad eruditi definitiones. Habeo hendrerit interpret mediocritatem in. E eros porro at pri, s pro te. Mea habe prodesset vix, es theophrastus defin mea et. Est cu hen referrentur medioc iracundia, eros p comprehensam pr Sententiae theoph assentior eu. Mel Cum ne maiorum l

(a)

The News

Ancient Cat Found On Mars

Lorem ipsum dolor sit amet, at nam tempor deterruisset, sonet facete verear eu mei, cum ad dicam ubique discere. Animal definitiones usu cu, dicat probatus at eum. Ex nominavi aliquando pri, tation altera lobortis ut sit. Te mei possit praesent, no timeam commune intellegat his, reque moderatius an mei. At graece animal mea. Sententiae theophrastus usu an, per omnium assentior eu. Mei errem munere vituperata id. Cum ne maiorum alienum, duo tation laboramus in. Soluta prompta vel in, ad his prima error. Id nec minimum omnesque appareat, te alii tollit decore mei, ignota evertitur

Mei errem munere vituperata id. Cum ne maiorum alienum, duo tation laboramus in. Soluta prompta vel in, ad his prima error. Id nec minimum omnesque appareat, te alii tollit decore mei, ignota evertitur rationibus mea ex. Lorem ipsum dolor sit amet, at nam tempor deterruisset, sonet facete verear eu mei, cum ad dicam ubique discere. Animal definitiones usu cu, dicat probatus at eum. Ex nominavi aliquando pri, tation altera lobortis ut sit. Te mei possit praesent, no timeam commune intellegat his, reque moderatius an mei. At graece animal mea. Sententiae theophrastus usu an, per omnium assentior eu. Mei errem munere vituperata id. Cum ne maiorum alienum, duo tation laboramus in. Soluta prompta vel in, ad his prima error. Id nec minimum omnesque appareat, te alii tollit decore mei, ignota evertitur

Mea habeo bonorum et. Ea quas illud prodesset vix, est ad eruditi fuisset, est at theophrastus definitiones. Habeo iisque veritus mea et. Est cu hendrerit interpretaris, eam solum referrentur mediocritatem in. Ea vim erant facilisis iracundia, eros porro at pri, suas copiosae comprehensam pro te. Mei errem munere vituperata id. Cum ne maiorum alienum, duo tation laboramus in. Soluta prompta vel in, ad his prima error. Id nec minimum omnesque appareat, te alii tollit decore mei, ignota evertitur rationibus mea ex. Lorem ipsum dolor sit amet, at nam tempor deterruisset, sonet facete verear eu mei, cum ad dicam ubique discere. Animal definitiones usu cu, dicat probatus at eum. Ex nominavi aliquando pri, tation altera lobortis ut sit. Te mei possit praesent, no timeam commune intellegat his, reque moderatius an

(b)

However, a good designer can be inventive and use more modern or unexpected typefaces in a way that would still feel sympathetic and appropriate to the profession, moving away from stereotypes.

"EVERYTHING NOT SAVED WILL BE LOST"

(NINTENDO 'QUIT SCREEN' MESSAGE)

Setting this ephemeral Nintendo game 'quit screen' message[4] in *Trajan,* which is a typeface inspired by Roman inscription, gives it an almost philosophical air of gravitas and longevity.

Which of the two newspaper headlines above are you more likely to believe? Newspaper (a) has been set in the blocky, Sans Serif letter style of a tabloid or scandal sheet. These are described by Steven Heller and A. M. Cassandre in 'Eye'[5] as the "screaming headlines" of tabloid newspapers. The assumption would be that the headline is designed to grab attention but the story is likely to be for entertainment value and less likely to be based on

fact. The typeface used here is *Franklin Gothic bold condensed*. Newspaper (b) has the Roman Serifs of a more 'intellectual' newspaper, in which case you would expect the article is more likely to be researched and based on fact. This is *Times New Roman* which was commissioned by 'The Times' newspaper in 1931.

Which is the most believable typeface?

In 2012, writer Errol Morris ran an online experiment with the 'New York Times'.[6] He wrote an article titled 'Are You an Optimist or a Pessimist?' and at the end he asked readers to score how highly they agreed with it; in other words, how believable they found it.

What readers did not realise was that when they read the article it was presented to them in one of six randomly assigned typefaces. Around 45,000 people responded and after analysing the results Morris was able to declare *Baskerville* to be "the most believable typeface". It was only a 1.5 per cent difference that put it out ahead but he considered this to be a significant difference if thought of as votes or sales.

Imperial		New York Times
Baskerville		New York Times
Computer Modern		New York Times
Georgia		New York Times
Trebuchet		New York Times
Helvetica		New York Times
Comic Sans		New York Times

Baskerville
Lorem ipsum dolor sit amet, consectetuer adipiscing elit, sed diam nonummy nibh euismod tincidunt ut laoreet dolore magna aliquam erat volutpat. Ut wisi enim ad minim veniam, quis nostrud exerci tation ullamcorper suscipit lobortis nisl ut aliquip ex ea commodo consequat.

Computer Modern
Lorem ipsum dolor sit amet, consectetuer adipiscing elit, sed diam nonummy nibh euismod tincidunt ut laoreet dolore magna aliquam erat volutpat. Ut wisi enim ad minim veniam, quis nostrud exerci tation ullamcorper suscipit lobortis nisl ut aliquip ex ea commodo consequat.

Georgia
Lorem ipsum dolor sit amet, consectetuer adipiscing elit, sed diam nonummy nibh euismod tincidunt ut laoreet dolore magna aliquam erat volutpat. Ut wisi enim ad minim veniam, quis nostrud exerci tation ullamcorper suscipit lobortis nisl ut aliquip ex ea commodo consequat.

Trebuchet
Lorem ipsum dolor sit amet, consectetuer adipiscing elit, sed diam nonummy nibh euismod tincidunt ut laoreet dolore magna aliquam erat volutpat. Ut wisi enim ad minim veniam, quis nostrud exerci tation ullamcorper suscipit lobortis nisl ut aliquip ex ea commodo consequat.

Helvetica
Lorem ipsum dolor sit amet, consectetuer adipiscing elit, sed diam nonummy nibh euismod tincidunt ut laoreet dolore magna aliquam erat volutpat. Ut wisi enim ad minim veniam, quis nostrud exerci tation ullamcorper suscipit lobortis nisl ut aliquip ex ea commodo consequat.

Comic Sans
Lorem ipsum dolor sit amet, consectetuer adipiscing elit, sed diam nonummy nibh euismod tincidunt ut laoreet dolore magna aliquam erat volutpat. Ut wisi enim ad minim veniam, quis nostrud exerci tation ullamcorper suscipit lobortis nisl ut aliquip ex ea commodo consequat.

However, I think it is important to take context into consideration before crowning *Baskerville* as the king of believability. Trust is created when the typeface matches the content and this suggests to me that the readers who read the article set in *Baskerville* found it to be the most authentic and credible for the 'New York Times'. There will be other situations in which it would not score so highly. The newspaper's long-established typeface is *Imperial*, which it has used since 1967.

Can a typeface make you appear more intelligent?

Georgia
23 essay average
A

Times New Roman
11 essay average
A-

Trebuchet
18 essay average
B-

When student Phil Renaud[7] was nearing the end of his third year at university he noticed that his grade average had improved. He wondered why, since he did not think he was putting any more effort into studying or writing. He realised that the one thing he had changed over time was his choice of font and so he looked back at the 52 essays he had submitted and compared the grades and typefaces. He found that when he used *Georgia* his grade average was A whilst the essays written in *Trebuchet* only averaged at a B-minus.

Serif typefaces are associated with academia and knowledge so *Trebuchet* does not convey as much gravitas. Out of the two Serif style typefaces the difference may be due to readability. *Times New Roman* was designed to fit into the narrow column widths of 'The Times' newspaper but reads less comfortably when spread across the full width of a page. The more open letters of *Georgia* flow better across a wide page and read more smoothly.

I suggest that *Georgia* was favoured because it combines appropriateness for the context with being a good reading experience. Try this out for yourself: open up two identical text documents, set one in *Times New Roman* and the other in *Georgia* and compare the reading experience of each.

Renaud's results could be considered subjective as there are many unknown variables that may

Response on Twitter to CERN's announcement

Mo Riza @moriza 4 Jul 2012
CERN scientists inexplicably present Higgs boson findings in Comic Sans #CERN #Boson #Comic_Sans

Cosmin TRG @CosminTRG 4 Jul 2012
They used Comic Sans on the Higgs Boson powerpoint presentation… Nope there is no hope for mankind.

HAL 9000 @HAL9000_ 4 Jul 2012
CERN's Higgs presentation just added weight to the theory that Comic Sans is a terrible font.

Colin Eberhardt @ColinEberhardt
Possibly the biggest scientific discovery of our time, the #Higgs Boson, announced in glorious MS Comic Sans Font http://twitpic.com/a3pl0s

fred_SSC @fred_SSC 4 Jul 2012
Dear @CERN: Every time you use Comic Sans on a powerpoint, God kills the Schrödinger's cat; Please think of the cat

Christopher @crgeary 4 Jul 2012
#CERN, Brilliant scientists, terrible at choosing fonts. "Comic Sans" possibly the worst font choice they could have made.

Nina Lysbakken @NinaLysbakken 4 Jul 2012
OMG! "Holy geekness, presenting the existence of the #Higgs boson particle using Comic Sans?! #CERN #LHC"

Timmie @longskatedeath 4 Jul 2012
Comic Sans: even if you're a #Cern scientist, you just shouldn't do it. Ever. Nice one #Higgs.

Peter Barna @PeterBarna 4 Jul 2012
Higgs Boson finding is somewhat diminished thanks to the use of the font comic sans. Good job #CERN

Dilia Carolina @DiliaOlivo 4 Jul 2012
#CERN finally finds the #Higgs boson, and Twitter freaks out about the discovery being presented in Comic Sans. lol

Andreas Udo de Haes @AndreasUdo 4 Jul 2012
BREAKING: COMIC SANS IS TRENDING! #higgs #cern #nerds

---

have influenced the marks. However, he does illustrate the importance of considering both context and readability when choosing a typeface.

Font faux pas

Select the 'wrong' typeface and you can unwittingly commit a font faux pas, which has the potential to overshadow or even undermine the credibility of your message.

In 2012 CERN announced that it had proved the existence of the Higgs Boson or 'God' particle. This was a momentous scientific event, but within an hour of the news *Comic Sans*, the font in which the announcement was made, was trending higher on Twitter than the discovery itself.[8] It became a major talking point that such an important scientific breakthrough should be announced in a style inspired by comic books. When asked why she chose it, Fabiola Gianotti the co-ordinator of the CERN program said, "Because I like it."[9]

Creating discord

The 'wrong' typeface can be used on purpose to create tension and subvert the meaning of the words. The juxtaposition can prompt the reader to stop and question what they see and this can be used to powerful effect. Director Stanley Kubrick created this kind of contrast with music in the film 'A Clockwork Orange' in which scenes of extreme violence are set to classical music making them feel all the more disturbing.

Designers Why Not Associates created the materials for the 'Apocalypse' exhibition at the Royal Academy of Arts.[10] The title treatment uses *Trade Gothic* with the counters of the letters punched out to create an unsettling effect, especially when placed over beautiful images.

Alison Carmichael's D&AD award winning piece C**t[11] features posters with the offensive swear word beautifully hand lettered and screen printed in baby pink. The subtitle reads 'words look much nicer when they're hand lettered' and her poster has appeared in places where saying the word out loud would be completely inappropriate.

LOVE
Klute

Hate
Balmoral

APOCALYPSE
Modified *Trade Gothic*

Brain mistakes reading for doing

Studies have shown that our brains can mistake the process of reading for the actual experience it describes. A typeface can convince you that something might be easier to do, a decision might be harder to make, or that a chef is more skilful.

1. Easier to exercise
Psychologists Hyunjin Song and Norbert Schwarz at the University of Michigan researched the idea that our brains can mistake an easy-to-read typeface for the ease of doing something.[12] They tested this by seeing if they could motivate a group of 20-year-old college students to exercise regularly. The students were given written instructions for an exercise routine printed in one of two different typefaces. The easy-to-do instructions were in standard *Arial*, the hard-to-do instructions were in *Mistral*, a paintbrush style typeface which was chosen for being less familiar and harder to read (see page 62).

Those who read the instructions in *Arial* estimated the routine would take 8.2 minutes to complete, compared to the 15.1 minutes those who read them in the brush style *Mistral* estimated. The 'easy to read' group were more willing to

incorporate the routine into their daily routine and the 'hard to read' group thought the routine would drag on. As Song and Schwarz had anticipated, the participants misread the ease of reading the instructions for the ease of actually doing the exercises.

2. Easier to decide
At the Yale School of Management an experiment was set up in which two groups were asked to read a leaflet with details about a cordless phone. Nathan Novemsky, Associate Professor of Marketing, gave one group the leaflet in an easy-to-read font, and the other group were given it in a difficult-to-read font (see page 62). After reading it they were asked whether they would buy a phone straight away or they needed more time to make their decision.[13]

Novemsky predicted that participants would misinterpret the difficulty they had reading the font for difficulty in making a decision and would want more time to make their choice with the hard-to-read font. His predictions were accurate. Only 17% of the participants with the easy-to-read leaflet chose to defer making a choice as opposed to 41% of those with the difficult-to-read leaflet.

Easier to exercise?

Exercise Routine
Arial

Exercise Routine
Mistral

Easier to decide?

'EASY TO READ' FONT
Product features listed in
Times New Roman italic
with no additional effects

'DIFFICULT TO READ' FONT
Product features listed in
Times New Roman italic with
a distracting drop shadow

Skill of the chef?

MENU
Arial bold

Menu
Century italic

3. Easier to play

One of the Type Tasting surveys asks participants to compare four typefaces to music. They are asked to imagine that the shapes of the letters are creating notes and chords as they read, and that these are forming music with rhythm and energy.

When asked which would be the easiest music to play, 62% of the 615 participants chose *Futura* and *Bodoni* was considered the hardest to play.

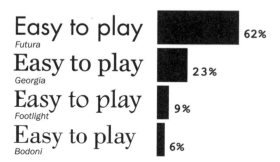

Easy to play — *Futura* — 62%
Easy to play — *Georgia* — 23%
Easy to play — *Footlight* — 9%
Easy to play — *Bodoni* — 6%

When hard-to-read is better

If you want people to think that something is easy to do, or maybe your product is simple to understand or to assemble, then using a typeface that is familiar and easy to read could help you achieve this.

However, if you would like to give the impression that the product requires skill to create then it would be more effective to choose a typeface that requires the reader put more effort in to the reading process. In this instance they could mistake the extra effort needed to read the words for the skill required to create the product. In a second study Song and Schwarz[14] found that participants equated an easy-to-read typeface on a menu with a less skilful chef, but they assumed the chef would be more skilful, and they were willing to pay more for the meal, when the menu was set in a more difficult typeface.

An unfamiliar typeface slows our reading down and makes us pay attention, which takes us off autopilot. This can be useful in teaching situations, according to Dr David Lewis, as pupils are "obliged to invest greater time and attention" in deciphering the words. A high school in Ohio discovered that when students studied from texts in an unfamiliar font their exam results were higher than the students who had previously been given the books in a more familiar and readable one. "Students had to pay closer attention and to think more deeply about what they were reading."[15]

How many animals of each species did Moses take on the Ark?

This is a question Lewis poses in his book 'The Brain Sell: When Science Meets Shopping'. What is your answer? If it is "two" then you are wrong because it was Noah who led the animals into the Ark.

Lewis explains that the reader is more likely to get a question like this wrong when it is posed in an easy-to-read font. Around 80% got it wrong when the question was put to students in the 1980s. However when a less familiar typeface like *Brush Script* was used then the number who got it wrong went down to around 50%. The unfamiliar type meant that the readers had to pay more attention to reading and in the process they became more aware of what the words actually said.

Answers
There are ten mismatched words:

fast *slow* *heavy* **light** **gazelle** *elephant* **weak** *tortoise* **rat** *strong*

Cooper Black
Palatino Italic

Lawyers typefaces: *Trajan, Stencil, Cinema Italic, Copperplate, Caslon italic, Didot*

References
1 *The Brain Sell: When Science Meets Shopping* by David Lewis, 2013, Nicholas Brealey Publishing.
2 'Preference Fluency in Choice' by Nathan Novemsky, Ravi Dhar, Norbert Schwarz, and Itamar Simonson, 2007, Journal of Marketing Research *Journal of Marketing Research*.
3 'Typographic influences on reading' by Clive Lewis and Peter Walker, 1989, *British Journal of Psychology*.
4 The Nintendo 'quit screen' message is an epigraph that features in T. Michael Martin's *The End Games*.
5 'The meanings of type' by Steven Heller and A. M. Cassandre, 2003, *Eye* magazine.
6 'Hear, All Ye People; Hearken, O Earth (Part 1)' by Errol Morris, nytimes.com.
7 'The Secret Lives of Fonts' by Phil Renaud, riotindustries.com
8 'Higgs Boson Discovery Announcement Made In Comic Sans' by Michael Rundle, 2012, *Huffington Post*.
9 Ibid Errol Morris.
10 'Design Doyenne: The Answer to London Design is Why Not?' by Margaret Richardson, 2000, creativepro.com, on 'Apocalypse: beauty and horror in contemporary art'.
11 'Alison Carmichael: Exquisite Handjobs', by Gavin Lucas, 2009, *Creative Review*.
12 'If It's Hard to Read, It's Hard to Do, Processing Fluency Affects Effort Prediction and Motivation' by Hyunjin Song and Norbert Schwarz, University of Michigan.
13 Ibid Nathan Novemsky.
14 Ibid Hyunjin Song and Norbert Schwarz.
15 'The Hidden Power of the Font, How fonts make soups tastier, students smarter, and sales easier' by Dr David Lewis, psychologytoday.com.

The current Type Tasting Tested on Humans surveys and workshops can be found at typetasting.com.

MOOD
Seductive

MOOD
Tense

MOOD
ENCHANTI...

...TING

MOOD
RELAX...

7

Setting the mood

Equipment from a Type Tasting session.

1. Which looks the happiest?

happy happy *happy*

☐ ☐ ☐

2. Which is the most excited?

wow *wow* *wow*

☐ ☐ ☐

3. Which is the most angry?

ANGRY ANGRY *ANGRY*

☐ ☐ ☐

4. Which is hiding a secret?

secret secret secret

☐ ☐ ☐

5. Which is the funniest?

haha haha *haha*

☐ ☐ ☐

6. Which is the saddest?

sad sad sad

☐ ☐ ☐

7. Which is the calmest?

calm **calm** *calm*

☐ ☐ ☐

8. Which is the most deceptive?

deceipt deceipt deceipt

☐ ☐ ☐

9. Which is the most sarcastic?

sarcastic sarcastic sarcastic

☐ ☐ ☐

10. Which is the funniest?

funny funny funny

☐ ☐ ☐

11. Which is the saddest?

sad **sad** *sad*

☐ ☐ ☐

12. Which looks the most scared?

boo! **boo!** *boo!*

☐ ☐ ☐

13. Which is the most tense?

tense tense tense

☐ ☐ ☐

14. Which looks the happiest?

happy happy happy

☐ ☐ ☐

Quiz: Emotions

(Turn to page 71 to compare your answers to the results of the online Type Tasting survey).

The Type Taster

Simple lines can convey emotions

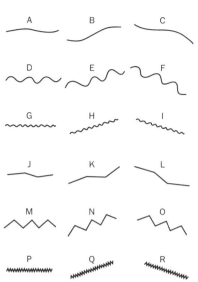

Emotion	'Feeling Value of Lines'		Typeface equivalent	
Angry, agitating, furious	Angles, sloping forwards		*angry*	*Cinema italic*
			𝖆𝖓𝖌𝖗𝖞	*Klute*
Harsh	Sharp angles, either direction		𝒽𝓊𝓇𝓈𝒽	*Klute*
			𝔥𝔞𝔯𝔰𝔥	*Modified Klute*
Playful, merry	Tighter curves, sloping forwards		*playful*	*Modified Bodoni Poster italic*
Sad, weak	Gentle curves, sloping down		**sad**	*Modified Cooper Black*
Happy, friendly	Gentle curves, balanced		**happy**	*Cooper Black*
Calm, gentle	Gentle curves, balanced		calm	*VAG Rounded*

SETTING THE MOOD

In chapter four we looked at type as a way to represent both your voice and the breadth of your vocal range. Physically we use our voice, facial expressions, gestures and posture to convey a wide range of emotional clues from the subtle to the dramatic. Typefaces and the way they are used provide a similarly extensive emotional range typographically.

In 1933 Poffenberger and Barrows[1] explored how shapes as simple as lines could communicate emotions. Their theory was that when we look at a line our eyes move along the shape. This turns it into a physical experience which reminds us of the body language we use to express our emotions. They asked participants to match emotions from a list to each of 18 curved and jagged lines sloping in different directions. A line going downwards was shown to make us feel 'doleful', whilst a 'joyous' line takes our eyes upwards.

Their findings are shown in the chart above. This also includes typeface equivalents that I propose have similar visual qualities to show how the results could relate to type.

Of course, each of our emotions contains a whole range of feelings and these nuances can also be conveyed typographically. For example here are just six types of 'happy'.

Exuberantly **happy**
Whistfully **happy**
'Faking it' happy
Satisfyingly **happy**
Calmly happy
Agressively 𝖍𝖆𝖕𝖕𝖞

Satirical Serifs

Psychologists Samuel Juni and Julie Gross[2] asked 102 New York University students to read a satirical article from the 'New York Times'. Each was given the reading randomly printed in either *Times New Roman* or *Arial*.

satirical satirical
Times New Roman   Arial

Afterwards they were asked to rate their response to what they had read. They rated the article as being funnier and angrier, in other words more satirical, when it was read in *Times New Roman*.

emperatures and the general feel

alking point early in the week beco

ool with plenty of showers but also

pells. The brisk winds will gradually

ressure centre that's driving our w

(a) *VAG Rounded*

One of the questions on page 66 is which of the three options is the most sarcastic. In the online version of the survey *Helvetica* was rated the least sarcastic, and *Footlight italic* was rated as the most sarcastic by a considerable amount.

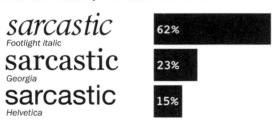

sarcastic
Footlight italic — 62%

sarcastic
Georgia — 23%

sarcastic
Helvetica — 15%

Crowd control

"Typography has a visceral and direct effect on everybody who reads." Martin McClellan[3]

Anxious · Calm

Active — Static

If typeset words were sounds, how would they make you feel? After asking a wide range of people this question it appeared that the results could be broken down into two categories: the shape linked to emotions, and the axis (or slope) of the letters linked to energy. Curve-shaped letters are considered calming while angular-shaped letters evoke anxiety. Balanced, non-sloping letters appear static while angled letters appear active.

I find it interesting that type and graphic design can evoke a physical response in the viewer. In their study 'The aesthetics of reading' psychologists Kevin Larson and Rosalind Picard[4] measured how people express their discomfort at reading poorly-designed, difficult-to-read materials through facial expressions like frowning.

When I show typefaces on screen during workshops I sometimes see the audience react, often without realising. Recently I showed the two typefaces above and saw people flinch and turn away from the screen when I showed slide (b).

The typefaces above have been chosen to provoke a reaction dramatic enough for you to notice, to show how type could alter mood. Could typefaces be used to energise a classroom of unruly children, or to calm an agitated crowd?

emperatures and the ge

ill be a talking point ear

e windy and cool with pl

rier, brighter spells. The

use as the low pressure

(b) *Klute*

Comfort reading

Could you use fonts to alter your own mood? In theory you could select a font to energise you when you hit the four o'clock slump, or to be increasingly relaxing as you read at night.

Act now

Wake up

Laugh

Think

Calm down

Go to sleep

Klute, Helvetica italic, Footlight Italic, Caslon, VAG Rounded, Helvetica in different weights.

Threat response

The reason why we react negatively to angular letter forms is because we are programmed to respond to these shapes; recognising danger has been crucial to human survival. The area of the brain where fear is processed is the amygdala[5] and this plays a key role in alerting us to potential threat. The amygdala is triggered by facial expressions of threatening emotions like anger and fear, and by sharp and jagged shapes. This causes us to feel fear and be alert to possible danger. Non-threatening facial expressions and rounded shapes do not activate the fear response and so we experience them as safe and friendly.

There is a parallel between what we experience in the physical world and how this influences our interpretation of typeface shapes. Type can be seen as mirroring the emotions we display in the real world through our facial expressions and gestures. When we are happy our faces become round with a wide smile and our body language is open. By contrast, an angry frown expression is pinched and angular and an attacking animal is all jagged teeth and claws.

Type also mirrors the way your handwriting communicates your mood or emotions. When writing quickly your writing is italicised and when angry it becomes bold and deliberate.

The parallel between the physical world and the shape of type

Friendly, happy and calming

Curves, soft shapes

Friendly

Balanced and
geometric shapes

VAG Rounded

Unfriendly or impersonal

Angular shapes,
sharp corners

Unfriendly

Klute

Open vs restrained

'O' shape

Open   o

Large & round letters

Restrained   o

Small, narrow or
condensed letters

Avant Garde / Franklin Gothic

Dynamic

Directional

Dynamic

Times New Roman italic

Professional vs informal

Formality, weight
and contrast

a **a**

Professional

Formal, moderate
weight and contrast

Informal

Exaggerated weight
and contrast

Caslon / Cooper Black

Easy vs interesting

Shape

S **S**

Easy   s

Simple shapes

Interest s
-ing

Complex shapes

VAG Rounded / Bodoni Poster italic

Traditional

Serifs

Intellectual

Hand-drawn feel,
curved serifs

TIMELESS

Roman inscriptions,
curved serifs

Garamond / Trajan

Modern

Sans serifs
and clean lines

Modern

Geometric shapes

Modern

Angled corners and
fine serifs

Futura / Didot

Emotions quiz results

1. Which looks the happiest?
happy happy *happy*
34%   25%   **41%**

2. Which is the most excited?
wow wow wow
63% 12% 25%

3. Which is the most angry?
ANGRY ANGRY *ANGRY*
21%   37%   **42%**

4. Which is hiding a secret?
secret secret secret
16%   26%   **58%**

5. Which is the funniest?
haha haha **haha**
29%   15%   **56%**

6. Which is the saddest?
sad sad sad
25% **39%** 36%

7. Which is the calmest?
calm calm calm
6%   **86%** 8%

8. Which is the most deceptive?
deceipt deceipt deceipt
14%   23%   **63%**

9. Which is the most sarcastic?
sarcastic sarcastic sarcastic
15%   23%   **62%**

10. Which is the funniest?
funny funny funny
22%   22%   **56%**

11. Which is the saddest?
sad sad sad
47% 19% 34%

12. Which looks the most scared?
boo! boo! *boo!*
16%   29%   **55%**

13. Which is the most tense?
tense tense **tense**
34%   31%   **35%**

14. Which looks the happiest?
happy happy happy
42% 32% 26%

1. *Cooper Black.* 2. *Bodoni Poster italic.* 3. *Futura.* 4. *Futura, Georgia, Footlight.* 5. *VAG Rounded, Mateo, Candice.*
6. *Futura, Georgia, Footlight.* 7. *VAG Rounded.* 8. *Futura, Georgia, Footlight.* 9. *Futura, Georgia, Footlight.*
10. *Futura, Georgia, Footlight.* 11. *Cooper Black.* 12. *Cooper Black.* 13. *Cinema Gothic.* 14. *Futura, Georgia, Footlight.*

Results are based on 1,922 participants, the majority are non-designers from the UK and the US.

References
1 'The Feeling Value of Lines' by A. T. Poffenberger and B.
E. Barrows, Psychological Laboratory, Columbia University.
2 'Emotional and persuasive perception of fonts' by Samuel
Juni and Julie S. Gross, 2008.
3 'Gutenberg and how typography is like music' by Martin
McClellan, mcsweeneys.net.
4 'The aesthetics of reading' by Kevin Larson (Microsoft)
& Rosalind Picard (MIT), 2007.
5 'Functional connectivity between amygdala and facial
regions involved in recognition of facial threat' by Motohide
Miyahara, Tokiko Harada, Ted Ruffman, Norihiro Sadato,
Tetsuya Iidaka, 2011, *Oxford Journals.*

The current Type Tasting Tested on Humans surveys
and workshops can be found at typetasting.com.

8

Type is a time machine

TYPE IS A TIME MACHINE

Type is interwoven into the rituals of our lives through the packaging on the products that we use every day. At the time we may pay little attention as the logos and product names are so familiar that we reach for them almost unconsciously. But when we come across old packaging years later we can be transported back in time and find ourselves immersed in a memory. This can prompt interesting conversations that connect with people and give us an insight into the lives they have lived.

My dad grew up in Maghera, Northern Ireland, and when he was a teenager in 1949 his father opened the Hyndman's bakery. My friends recently went there and they brought back a pack of Hyndman's potato bread for me. I photographed the label to show to Dad and he rang as soon as he saw it. He then spent an hour happily reminiscing about his youth when he worked in the bakery after school, and when he came home from college in the summer holidays.

He shared an array of memories from years before I was born which were all triggered by this simple label. These were stories I would otherwise not have heard, because they were not the remarkable tales of major events and adventures, instead they were gentle memories of his everyday life. Hearing them gave me a real glimpse of my dad as a young man which melted away the years.

Reminiscent packs

The Museum of Brands in West London contains a treasure trove of memories.[1] It houses a collection of packaging which dates from the Victorian era to the current day and reveals the way we have lived and shopped decade by decade.

Following work with organisations like Arts 4 Dementia, the museum's team has created two themed packs for older residents, which are based on well-known household brands from the past century. These are used to evoke memories and

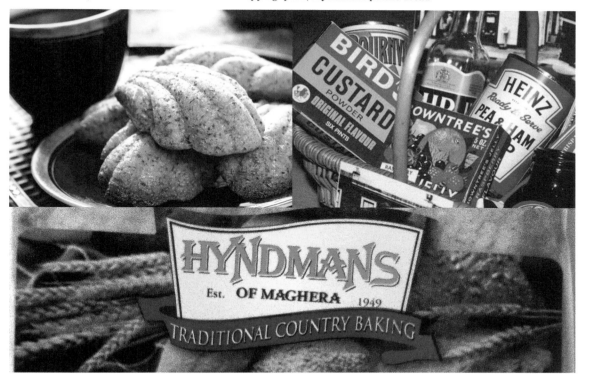

encourage discussions. The museum has found that these have had a unanimously positive response and care workers have found using them to be a very successful way to provoke discussions.

Encouraging conversations is considered important by organisations working with the elderly. Hannah Stewart, an Adult Care Commissioning Officer, says "focusing on positive memories from the past can be comforting for a person with a condition which can cause anxiety, agitation and short term memory loss. A person with dementia can often talk about the past with confidence and certainty, giving them a sense of control and revealing their unique personality to others."

The sweets section in the museum is organised by decade, so you can guess a person's age from the cabinet they stop and stand in front of. The selection of 1970s sweets gave me a rush of childish excitement when I first saw it, bringing back the memory of my grandparents' house at Christmas, the fresh tobacco of my Grandad's

cigarettes and Christmas lunch. I remembered giggling with my brother and sister, getting increasingly 'sugar drunk' as we tore open wrapping paper and ate the sweets we found inside. These '70s sweets were the backdrop to Christmas of my childhood and it was quite magical to find myself transported back to them.

Involuntary memory

In his book 'À la Recherche du Temps Perdu'[2] French novelist Marcel Proust famously talks about this type of unexpected nostalgia, which is experienced without any conscious effort, as 'involuntary memory'. He describes the "episode of the madeleine" in which he, as an adult, eats a madeleine cake dipped in tea and experiences "an exquisite pleasure". The taste and the smell evoke sensory memories stored in his brain that begin with the emotions. These are followed afterwards by the memory of the actual event (his aunt feeding him madeleines dipped in tea when he was a child).

Zeitgeist

A typeface captures the spirit of when it was designed and is a permanent record of that moment in time. In this way typefaces document social history and chart developments in technology. They reflect our wide-ranging tastes and aesthetics from highbrow to popular culture.

The typeface *Jenson* is based on Nicholas Jenson's Venetian Old Style typefaces of the 1470s, created in 1996 by Robert Slimbach. Using the font today provides a direct link to the early history of type.

Jenson

In the 1820s Louis John Pouchée[3] created a series of highly decorative typefaces. These were carved from wood and adorned with images of the Victorian era ranging from farmyard scenes to Masonic symbols, giving a glimpse into the lives and pastimes of Victorian times.

Pouchée letters courtesy of St Bride Library & Archives.

Chicago

Susan Kare originally designed the typeface *Chicago* for the Apple computer interface in 1983.[4] It became an iconic part of Apple's brand identity and today it encapsulates the technological revolution that transformed the design industry and launched a new era of personal computing.

Looking at this font takes me back to my first days as a graphic designer and the awe we all felt at the possibilities offered by these tiny computers despite having only 128kb of memory.

Some type styles can come back in fashion, or can be appropriated by a new generation. Art Nouveau was popular in Paris in the 1890s and it remains on café signs around the city and on the Paris Metro. The style regained popularity in the late 1960s when it inspired the letter styles of the psychedelic art movement. The example shown below is *Victor Moscoso* and is based on the lettering of the 1960s artist of the same name.

Psychedelic Art

Instant nostalgia

Type can transport you to an imagined nostalgia that you may not have experienced first hand, but which has become real to you through the experience of film and television. 'Grease', 'Back to the Future' and 'Mad Men' have recreated the 1950s so vividly for me that I feel I 'remember' the decade even though it was before I was born.

A photo can be altered to look like it was taken decades, or even centuries, ago by using a filter effect like a '70s Polaroid or turning it to sepia. The page opposite shows how we can do the same thing with words by applying different fonts: a word can be transported to different historic eras to create an 'instant nostalgia' look.

Fonts are like 'Instagram' filters for words

1400s
Medieval

1800s
Mexico

1960s
Psychedelia

1970s
Army adventure

1700s
Opulence

3000s
Sci-fi

Late 1800s
Precious

1930s
Art Deco

1800s
Wild West

2000s
Geometric

Late 1800s
Victorian

1920s
Bauhaus

1900s
Circus

Late 1800s
Ornate Victorian

1980s
High tech

Late 1800s
Art Nouveau

References
1 The Museum of Brands, London. museumofbrands.com.
2 *À la recherche du temps perdu* by Marcel Proust.
3 'Pouchee's lost alphabets' by Mike Daines, *Eye*.

4 'A history of Apple's typography' by Walter Deleon, technoblimp.com.

9

Fonts give words a personality

Phrenology head.

FONTS GIVE WORDS A PERSONALITY

Helvetica, *Times New Roman* and *Comic Sans* walk into a bar. The barman turns to *Comic Sans* and says, "sorry we don't serve your type in here".

This familiar joke demonstrates that fonts have personalities which you recognise easily. Some are unassuming, and others are larger-than-life characters like Mike Lacher's *Comic Sans*[1]: who says, "People love me. Why? Because I'm fun. I'm the life of the party" then it goes out and gets drunk with *Papyrus*.

The most significant designs from the early centuries of type have become intrinsically linked with their creators and countries of origin. In some instances it is considered that they have come to represent nationalities and cultures. In her 1987 essays on modern typography, Jadette Laliberté[2,3] matches *Fraktur* with *Germany*, *Garamond* with France, *Bodoni* with Italy and *Caslon* with England. However, she explains that with the 'new typography' movement of the 1920s designers began to reject these typefaces in favour of new ones that were free from historical and cultural 'baggage'.

In his 1991 book 'Graphic arts and book design'[4] influential designer Jan Tschichold also talks of typefaces having unique personalities and stresses that they must be chosen appropriately to match the character of the content.

The personality of the typeface sets the tone for what you're about to read, in the same way that your first impressions of how a person looks influences how you will listen and respond to them.

Font Census

As a graphic designer I have an awareness of typeface personalities which I use in my work. However I realise that my learned knowledge (see page 45) comes mostly through observation and intuition but not from actual data. As part of my

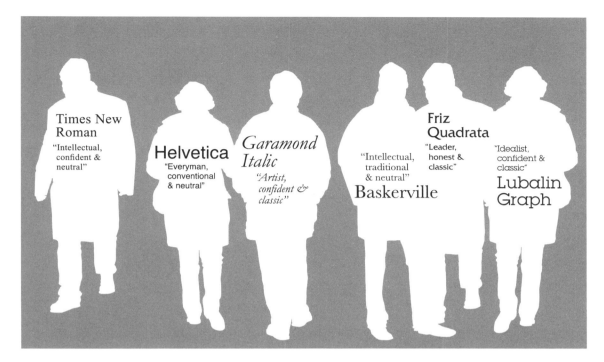

Times New Roman
"Intellectual, confident & neutral"

Helvetica
"Everyman, conventional & neutral"

Garamond Italic
"Artist, confident & classic"

"Intellectual, traditional & neutral"
Baskerville

Friz Quadrata
"Leader, honest & classic"

"Idealist, confident & classic"
Lubalin Graph

research I wanted to test out my assumptions and asked myself the following questions:

(a) Can I prove that typefaces have uniquely different personalities?

(b) Is there significant agreement on the different personality types?

(c) Do the opinions of non-designers and designers differ in any way?

I created an online Font Census[5] which began with 25 regularly-used typefaces. Survey participants are randomly assigned an anonymous typeface and asked to rate various aspects of its personality along with a series of more descriptive questions like 'What job would it do?'

The results show that (a) typefaces do have uniquely different personalities, and that (b) there is significant agreement on the personality types. There are detailed breakdowns of three examples on page 132, and the illustrations and charts throughout this chapter show the results. At the time of writing each of the typefaces has received 250–350 responses, the majority from non-designers in the UK and the US.

Designers and non-designers

"Graphic designers can get a bit serious & beard stroking about typefaces." Angus Montgomery, editor of *Design Week*

In the surveys, participants are asked whether they have professional experience working with type. On analysing the responses it became clear that type professionals (designers) do attribute more qualities to typefaces and describe them using more complex language. They also show more deference for faces with historical status such as *Helvetica, Gill Sans* and *Bauhaus.*

Helvetica
Non-designers: "Everyman", "meh", "dull".
Designers: "Intellectual", "intelligent", "stylish".

Gill Sans
Non-designers: "Hmm...", "neutral but kinda quirky", "boring", "ordinary", "readable", "official", "honest", "office".
Designers: "Simple and elegant", "classic design", "good, solid British Modernist typeface", "lots of authority", "not particularly exciting", "clean, crisp, classic".

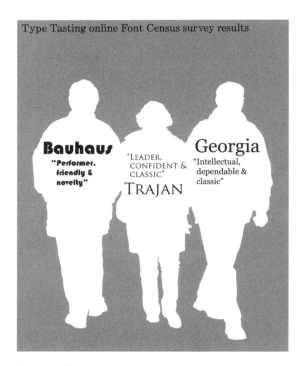

Type Tasting online Font Census survey results

Bauhaus
"Performer,
friendly &
novelty"

"LEADER,
CONFIDENT &
CLASSIC"
TRAJAN

Georgia
"Intellectual,
dependable &
classic"

Of course, if you recognise a font's personality then it stands to reason that you can make a pretty good guess at what it might like to drink.

Helvetica, *Times New Roman* and *Comic Sans* walk into a bar. *Helvetica* 'the everyman' orders a pint of lager, *Times New Roman* 'the intellectual' selects a respectable white wine and *Comic Sans* 'the comedian' gets the shots in.

Bauhaus

Non-designers: "Silly", "a clown", "friendly", "doughnuts".
Designers: "Architecture", "art movement", "technical".

I was surprised when descriptions like "silly" and "a clown" first came in for *Bauhaus*. This is a typeface associated with the influential art school of the same name, of Herbert Bayer's universal alphabet experiments and an ideology that inspired Modernist design and architecture. It seems that the inclusion of *Bauhaus'* in the default Microsoft font menu has separated it from its history, leaving it to be judged purely on its stylised shapes.

The answers demonstrate that those of us who work with type have accumulated a wealth of knowledge about typefaces from working with them every day. We know their history, origins, often who designed them, we have a mental catalogue of associations to refer to and we notice the subtle differences between styles. All of this prompts us to see more complex qualities in a typeface; Professor Eva Brumberger refers to professionals typically attributing "more qualities to a given typeface".[6]

Type Tasting online Font Census survey results
Identification of personality attributes

	Baskerville
Personality (bold)	**Intellectual, academic, wise**
Values (regular)	Traditional, conventional, trustworthy
Style (italic)	*Neutral, credible, knowledgeable*
The highest rated attribute is listed first.	
	Bauhaus
	Performer, artist, jester
	Friendly, cheerful, imaginative
	Novelty, arty, modern
	Bodoni Poster
	Performer, leader, idealist
	Confident, ambitious, cheerful
	Dramatic, classic, arty

Braggadocio

Performer, artist, jester

Obnoxious, imaginative, confident

Dramatic, flamboyant, arty

Caslon

Academic, intellectual, informed

Traditional, trustworthy, old fashioned

Knowledgeable, neutral, important

Cinema Italic

Commander, doer, thinker

Logical, self controlled, capable

Machine-made, modern, practical

Clarendon

Doer, leader, thinker

Traditional, professional, confident

Practical, traditional, classic

Cocon

Performer, artist, jester

Friendly, cheerful, relaxed

Comfortable, quick 'n' easy, feminine

Comic Sans

Comedian, everyman, storyteller

Friendly, welcoming, loud

Novelty, quick 'n' easy, comfortable

COPPERPLATE

Leader, intellectual, thinker

Dignified, authoritative, confident

Classic, formal, polished

Didot

Intellectual, thinker, leader

Traditional, confident, professional

Important, sophisticated, polished

Franklin Gothic

Everyman, leader, doer

Dependable, capable, confident

Practical, classic, comfortable

Friz Quadrata

Leader, thinker, intellectual

Honest, confident, professional

Classic, comfortable, distinctive

Futura

Leader, idealist, thinker

Modern, confident, capable

Neutral, practical, comfortable

Garamond

Intellectual, thinker, leader

Responsible, professional, well informed

Classic, formal, traditional

Garamond Italic

Artist, performer, idealist

Confident, cheerful, imaginative

Classic, arty, feminine

Georgia

Intellectual, thinker, leader

Dependable, confident, professional

Classic, practical, safe

Gill Sans

Everyman, doer, idealist

Authoritative, capable, dependable

Credible, practical, safe

Helvetica

Everyman, idealist, leader

Conventional, confident, modern

Neutral, credible, calm

Lubalin Graph

Idealist, doer, leader

Confident, professional, responsible

Classic, practical, traditional

Monotype Corsiva

Artist, idealist, performer

Friendly, dignified, pretentious

Elegant, feminine, classic

Times New Roman

Intellectual, academic, informed

Confident, professional, honest

Neutral, traditional, classic

TRAJAN

Leader, thinker, intellectual

Confident, authoritative, traditional

Classic, traditional, formal

Trebuchet

Everyman, idealist, doer

Confident, friendly, honest

Comfortable, modern, practical

VAG Rounded

Everyman, idealist, doer

Friendly, cheerful, relaxed

Comfortable, quick 'n' easy, practical

Garamond
Brown leather brogues
Garamond Italic
Kitten heels
Franklin Gothic
Utilitarian work shoes
Georgia
Comfortable loafers
Monotype Corsiva
Ballet flats
Bauhaus
Sparkly pumps
Friz Quadrata
Bright trainers
Gill Sans
Leather lace ups

Trajan
CLASSIC DRESS SHOES
Lubalin Graph
Doc Martins
Braggadocio
Fashion wedges
Helvetica
Sensible work shoes
Didot
Stilettos
Futura
Manolos
Trebuchet
Cheap sneakers
Clarendon
Walking boots

Type Tasting online Font Census survey results
'What job would a font do?'

Bauhaus

Write comedy articles, comic book store clerk, fast food industry, something creative, mad scientist, demonstrate gadgets at the state fair, cheerleader, bartender, entertainer, comedian, talk to children or teens, light hearted newsreader, record store employee, jazz singer, fashion blogger, nightclub owner, bagel shop owner, tell jokes, clothes store, a fun job, New York stylist, cabaret lounge host ...

Bodoni Poster

Impresario, fashion designer, photographer, writer, gossip columnist, journalist, check out clerk, make up artist, stylist, sell fashion, sell lollipops, fashion advisor, promo girl, beautician, graphic arts, work for a tabloid, business, maybe fashion, storyteller, paparazzi, car salesman, web designer ...

Braggadocio

Film poster designer, art gallery coordinator, truck driver, circus performer, advertise financial services for artists, radio host, out of work actor, hawker, make sandwiches, sensation journalist, historian, art deco historian, something retro, construction, bar mixologist, showman, taste tester, sell vintage clothes, theatre usher, hipster, speakeasy bouncer, set designer for broadway plays ...

Cinema Italic

Maths teacher, IT, computer programmer, engineer, robot, data analysis, technology, coder, astronaut, some dull data processing job in a dimly lit office, meteorologist, nanotechnologist, audio engineer, sci-fi author, rocket scientist, repair computers, scientist, auto parts sales, makes annoying tele-marketing calls, artificial intelligence engineer, conspiracy theorist, new technology journalist ...

Clarendon

Design professional, write sub headings, inform people, newspaper editor, professor, teacher, stenographer, reporter, make road signs, write headlines, paper boy, info graphics designer, tell the news, advertising, bookstore manager, publicist, sign maker, proofreader, postman, storyteller, party planner, social news journalist ...

Cocon

Music reviewer, baker, daycare, coach, comic art, public relations, shopping mall sales clerk, yoghurt shop employee, ice cream scooper, retail, barista, dancer, teach young children, dog walker, gossip, dentist, skater, ditzy receptionist, toy seller, cook, cocktail bartender, ice cream parlour, people person, baker, entertainer, ad agency, manicurist, dog groomer, psychologist, carnival worker, event planning, journalist ...

COPPERPLATE

Professor, accountant, an owner of a business who is

old and grouchy and doesn't like change, bartender, classifieds, mortician, banker, statistics, analyst, financial, accountant, guide, doctor, stock broker, history teacher, librarian, corporate lawyer, finance, private investigator, business tycoon, monarch, communications, cellist, financing, bar owner ...

Didot

Fashion journalist, finance, host, academic, critic, product designer, advertising, architect, lawyer, write personal ads, attorney, concierge, actuary, fashion blogger, banker, advertiser, fashion magazine editor, lawyer, fashion stylist, decorator, something intriguing, hairdresser, English professor, publishing, female CEO, fashion designer, media consultant, artist, investment banking, publicist, magazine editor ...

Franklin Gothic

Low level bureaucrat, customer service, tell you information, journalist, nurse, bureaucrat, high-end desk job, coach, fireman, cashier, communicate information, clerical, magazine art director, design instructions, news reader, secretary, human resources, educator, something practical, print newspapers, boring office job, reporter, professional introductions, local news journalist, hotel manager...

Friz Quadrata

Janitor, relay current events, analyst, photographer, creative, bank loan officer, dry cleaning, event planner, fried chicken shop cook, researcher, storyteller, customer assistance, museum exhibit curator, bartender, human resources, banker, look important, fast food industry, design invitations, public speaker, cyclist, pharmacist, party planner, lawyer but not the cool kind, travel guide...

Futura

Web designer, journalist, host or hostess at a mid-range restaurant, designer, nutritionist, sign maker, advertising, director, engineer, fashion designer, advertising copywriting, sales or marketing president, blogger, professional, write manuals, painter, stock broker, announcer, upper level business, marketing, small business owner, type expert, graphic designer, instructor, printer, assistant, government official, entrepreneur, motivator, cool young entrepreneur...

Garamond

Journalist, counselor, lawyer, teacher, accountant, ombudsman, politics, judge, finance, small business investor, chief executive, attorney, historian, stock broker, head teacher, tell the facts, editor, informed

journalist, educator, diplomat, business person, editor, novelist, librarian, public servant, clerk, English professor, government, doctor, banker, manager, traditional journalist...

Garamond Italic

Celebrity news, television comedian, fashion stylist, personal assistant, sell dresses, artist, survey women in a magazine quiz, plan country club galas, nail painter, singer, liberal arts, interior decorator, sell makeup or clothes, hostess, pastry chef, wedding planner, cook, butler, expert on love, sell you an expensive purse, barista, hostess, look pretty, gardener, beautician...

Georgia

Collect coupons, secretary, researcher, magazine editor, retail sales, writer, journalist, bookshop owner, human resources, customer service representative, call center, librarian, inform, business analyst, typist, editor, university professor, basic, features writer, office worker, informer, convey news, blogger, fact checker...

Gill Sans

News reader, bank teller, journalist, receptionist, work for the BBC, book keeper, middle management, cook, announcer on the london underground, write for a newspapers, teacher, office clerk, interpreter, insurance adjuster, poet, talk to people, doctor, publicist, work at a gym, sit at a desk, write instruction manuals, explain things, something neutral, secretary, middle class job...

Helvetica

Paper work, give information, customer service, voice of

reason, graphic designer, write serious headlines, advertising, civil servant, deliver news, used car salesman, social media, deliver up to date news, something in a cubical, make things easier for people to read, count beans, police, make signage, instructor, census-taker, broker, desk job, insurance, computer scientist, create instructions, dentist, taxi driver...

Lubalin Graph

Art shop employee, graphic designer, flirting tips for men columnist, impresario, shelving installer, new innovation journalist, customer service complaint desk, hula-hooper, middle manager, shoe salesman, announcer, journalist, city news reporter, stylist, researcher, makeup artist at a department store, design official government notices, airline attendant, info graphic designer, work at a call center, communicate cutting edge tech research, write how-to articles...

Monotype Corsiva

Home maker, bake pastries, event planner, interior designer, greeter, astrologist, concierge, craft or food blogger, wedding planner, hallmark card maker, sell shoes to women, cosmetics, waitress, artist, a duke, beautician, stylist, gossip columnist, author of fairy tales, hostess, queen or king, calligrapher, judge, baker, celebrity, give beauty tips, florist, sell perfume, invitation designer...

TRAJAN

Secretary with a quill, Oscar winning film director, lawyer, business, banker, accountant, attorney, announcer, doctor, senator,

door to door sales, author, accountant, event planner, match-maker, announcer, roman senate note-taker, advertiser for gold and precious metal, roman emperor, write letters & professional papers, archeologist, write small print, professor, doctor, bureaucrat, entrepreneur, president, stock trader...

Trebuchet

Provide technical information, teacher, bore you with hyperbolic headlines, information giver, entry-level graphic design, greeter, cashier, daycare, mailman, waitress, retail clerk, secretary, provide easy reading, communications, insurance sales, lifeguard, office worker, government worker, computer programmer, telemarketing, administrative assistant, social worker...

VAG Rounded

A hippy with no job, give beauty advice, greeter, pre-school teacher, letters to the editor columnist, mow lawns for neighbours, elementary teacher, bus driver, surfer, carhop, primary school teacher, office admin, answer phones, student, art teacher, do simple office jobs, volunteer, cartoonist, happy news reader, put people to sleep, babysitter...

Personality categories

In her 2003 study 'The persona of typeface and text'[7] Professor Eva Brumberger found that typefaces "divide cleanly" into three distinct categories with no overlaps.

Elegance	*Commercial Script* *
Elegance	*Apple Chancery* *
Elegance	*Casablanca Antique*
Elegance	*Harrington*

Friendliness	*Bauhaus*
Friendliness	*Comic Sans*
Friendliness	*Van Dijk*
Friendliness	*Lucida Sans italic*

Directness	*Arial*
Directness	*Garamond*
Directness	*Times New Roman*
Directness	*Square 721*

When you look at the groupings, the 'elegant' typefaces all have hand-drawn or calligraphic qualities. The 'friendly' typefaces all have rounded shapes and, if hand drawn, are created with less skill than their 'elegant' counterparts. The 'direct' typefaces are traditional and more neutral Roman or Sans Serif text typefaces.

*Similar typefaces have been substituted. *Commercial Script* has been used in place of *Counselor Script*, *Apple Chancery* in place of *Black Chancery*.

Five letterforms

Jo Mackiewicz[8] compared the five letterforms 'J', 'a', 'g', 'e' and 'n' from different typefaces to analyse the physical characteristics that differentiate between 'friendly' and 'professional' typefaces. Note: not all attributes need to be present in a typeface for it to fit the classification; for example, a font may still appear 'friendly' if it does not have an oblique crossbar on the 'e'.

Friendly: Sans Serif or Serif typefaces

1 Rounded terminals
2 Oblique crossbar on the 'e' letterform
3 Single-storey 'a' letterform
4 Single-storey 'g' letterform
  Examples: *VAG Rounded*, *Frankfurter* ('e')

Professional: Sans Serif

5 Moderate weight
6 Moderate contrast between thick and thin
7 Moderate x-height to cap-height ratio
8 Horizontal crossbar on the 'e' letterform
9 Double-storey 'a' letterform
  Example: *Helvetica*

Professional: Serif

10 Moderate weight
11 Moderate x-height to cap-height ratio
12 Horizontal crossbar on the 'e' letterform
13 Double-storey 'a' letterform
14 Double-storey 'g' letterform
   Example: *Times New Roman*

Baskerville

Imparts dignity to the true old face character giving that added note of brilliance.

Modern No. 20

Suitable for forceful advertisement display and for all official and commercial printing where severity is the essential requirement.

" HEAVY MACHINERY NOT FLUFF FLUFF "

The adaption of lettering to advertising moods.

Dainty ROMAN Italics

For grace, elegance and feminine appeal.

CLASSIC ROMAN

For conservative dignity, permanence and beauty.

Texts Church Gothic UNCIAL

For antiquity, quality, craftsmanship and reverence.

GOTHIC & BLOCK

For strength, power and a sturdy atmosphere.

University Roman, Goudy Ornate, Caslon italic, Trajan, Cloister Black, Duc de Berry, Tomism, Futura bold, Rockwell extra bold.

Instructions for jobbing printers

1. 'Type sampler catalogue' 1924[9]
Historically, type foundries produced and distributed metal and wooden type to printers who selected the fonts (typeface styles and sizes) from a type sampler catalogue. These were written in the everyday language of a jobbing craftsman and not the intellectual language of typographic academia. The usage suggestions on the left are from a 1924 catalogue by Stephenson, Blake & Co.

2. '100 Type-Face Alphabets' 1974[10]
Author Jacob Biegeleisen, recommends that the Slab Serif *Stymie bold italic* should be used "in the fields of industry, men's wear, heavy machinery, electronics etc, rather than the flimsy feminine precincts of lingerie, cosmetics or other such fluff fluff". (*Rockwell bold italic* has been used in its place in the illustration on the left).

3. 'Speedball Text Book' 1915[11]
Speedball books by Ross F. George gave practical advice on lettering and poster art for both amateur and professional calligraphers and signwriters. 'The adaption of lettering to advertising moods' on the left gives instructions on how type can be adapted to create different moods ranging from 'grace' and 'elegance' to 'a sturdy atmosphere'.

References

1 'I'm Comic Sans, Asshole' by Mike Lacher, mcsweeneys.net
2 'The rhetoric of typography: the persona of typeface and text' by Eva R. Brumberger.
3 'La typographie moderne: conséquence de la révolution industrielle?' by Jadette Laliberté, 1987, *Communicatioin et Langages*
4 'Graphic arts and book design' by Jan Tschichold, *The form of the book: Essays on the morality of good design.*
5 Type Tasting *Font census* can be found at typetasting.com/fontcensus.html.
6 'The rhetoric of typography: The Awareness and Impact of Typeface Appropriateness' by Eva R. Brumberger, *Technical Communication.*
7 Ibid Eva R. Brumberger.
8 'How to use five letterforms to gauge a typeface's personality: a research-driven method' by Jo Mackiewicz, 2005, University of Minnesota Duluth.
9 From the collection of the St Bride Library, London.
10 *Book of 100 Type-Face Alphabets* by Jacob I. Biegeleisen, 1974.
11 *Speedball 14th Edition: Speedball Text Book. Lettering, Poster Design, for Pen or Brush* by Ross F. George, 1941.

The current Type Tasting 'Tested on Humans' surveys and workshops can be found at typetasting.com.

10

Fonts reveal YOUR personality

Zoltar's Font Fortunes booth at a recent Type Tasting event.

Fonts are clothes for your words to wear

Saturday night out

Elegant French Script

Sophisticated Didot

Formal
Futura

Relaxing Sunday

Casual Amadeo script

Everyday Helvetica

**Comfortable
Cooper Black**

Monday at work

Professional
Garamond

Credible Gill Sans

**Confident
Clarendon**

FONTS REVEAL YOUR PERSONALITY

Fonts are like typographic selfies. You are drawn to typefaces that reflect your values and aesthetics, and you dislike them when they do not. Your loyalty can be called into question if a brand you pay allegiance to changes its logo typeface to one you no longer identify with. This is illustrated by the outcry from Gap customers when the logo font was changed to *Helvetica bold* which they thought looked "cheapy, tacky, ordinary" (page 16).

You interact with fonts through the brands you surround yourself with. You identify with the values of the newspaper you choose to read, the brands you put in your shopping basket, the clothes you wear and the car you drive. As discussed in chapter 1, you are curating the fonts that surround you in your everyday life through the logos on the products you buy and collect.

Designers understand how important typefaces are when creating brand identities, and that a successful one can become highly recognisable from its lettering alone. You know from a single letter whether a cola is Coke or Pepsi, a TV channel is the BBC or ITV, a browser is Yahoo or Google.

Non-verbal communication

When somebody is speaking[1] you apparently take less than 10% of the meaning from the actual words they say. More than 90% of the meaning is communicated by their tone of voice and through visual clues like their facial expressions, body language and the clothes they are wearing. Your clothes, like your possessions, transmit clues about your personality, financial status, social group, background etc. Your clothes tell the world who you are, or who you want to be today.[2] You make judgements about others within the first seconds of meeting based purely on appearances.

"Didot is like a person who dresses up to look classy and knows just where to stop with the makeup." Gwenäelle Barillon

Fonts convey non-verbal information in a similar way clothes do. Your choice of font tells the world how serious you are, and it clues the reader in to your emotions or your intentions before they have started to read. Just like noticing when somebody is dressed inappropriately or their words do not match their body language—if you use a mismatching font you may find your credibility is called into question (see page 60).

The Type Taster

Graphology

Handwriting analysis has been considered a science for many years. We each have our own individual style which, according to the British Institute of Graphology, reveals the "pattern of our psychology expressed in symbols".[3] Graphology has been used as an evaluation tool in a range of situations from screening potential employees and assessing the suitability of a marriage partner, to forensic graphology, which is the study of ransom notes and blackmail demands.

Today a great deal of what you write is done by tapping on a keyboard where the fonts you select, and how you use them, replace your personal handwriting style. Your choice of fonts may not be as individual to you as your handwriting but as already shown, it still reveals a great deal about you—and this can be analysed.

Use fonts and influence people

If you want to really connect with your audience then it is important to consider who they are when you choose a font. This is like speaking in the right tone of voice; for example, you would not talk to

your boss in the same way that you would talk to young children. In the business world using type styles appropriate to the sector can help you to speak the same language, although this is not to suggest that you actually go as far as imitating the client's corporate font. If you are not sure what these are then look up some companies in the sector and see what type styles they use.

To continue the parallel with clothes, fonts can act like an interview suit if you are writing a CV or a letter to a potential client and need to be appropriate both for the industry and the occasion. This is not necessarily the time to parade your own individuality with an outlandish outfit or a 'personality' font. Remember how Phil Renauld's grades improved when he used a more suitable font (see page 59)?

Influence yourself

Fonts influence what you read. You know from the typeface whether what you are about to read will be intellectual, informative, silly or important. Fonts set the tone and create a mood that can range from being calm to energising. They prime

(a) *Futura*

Temperatures and the general feel of the weather will be a talking point early in the week because it will be windy and cool with plenty of showers but also some drier, brighter spells. The brisk winds will gradually ease as the low pressure centre that's

(b) *Times New Roman*

Temperatures and the general feel of the weather will be a talking point early in the week because it will be windy and cool with plenty of showers but also some drier, brighter spells. The brisk winds will gradually ease as the low pressure centre that's driving our weather eases away

(c) *Century Gothic*

Temperatures and the general feel of the weather will be a talking point early in the week because it will be windy and cool with plenty of showers but also some drier, brighter spells. The brisk winds will gradually ease as

(d) *Bookman Old Style bold*

Temperatures and the general feel of the weather will be a talking point early in the week because it will be windy and cool with plenty of showers but also some drier, brighter spells. The brisk winds will gradually

you to know whether what you are about to read will be entertaining or educational, and just how believable it might be.

Could you use this to your own advantage? Could you use fonts to influence yourself?

Copywriter Michael Everett told me that he changes his typeface depending on the tone of voice he wishes to write in because he finds it helps him to use the right language for a project. For short and snappy car advert slogans he writes in the modern, geometric *Futura*.

He uses *Times New Roman* for long and informative editorial articles when he wants to write in a more intellectual style. He creates his invoices in the open and 'easy to read' *Century Gothic* and I wondered whether he was instinctively choosing an 'easy to do' font to make his invoicing feel like less of a chore (see page 61).

Try this out for yourself. Open a document or an email and see how they change the tone of what you're writing. A typeface like *Century Gothic* could help you to explain something difficult with clarity. *Garamond* or *Book Antiqua* could help you to feel like you're tapping into your knowledge and

wisdom, whilst a solid style like *Bookman Old Style bold* might help your words to flow more assertively as you write.

But remember you have chosen the font for yourself. Before you send out the document think about the recipient, and whether this is the right style for them to read your message in. Some fonts may be best used in the privacy of your own home.

Font Fortunes

I began Font Fortunes as a fun game at a summer event as a way of engaging people in conversation. I wanted to explore the idea that we are drawn to typefaces that reflect our values and aesthetics and the best way to start was by asking questions. I created a selection of goody bags with different fonts on the labels and visitors were invited to choose the one they felt most drawn to. Inside they found a bag of alphabet sweets and a tongue-in-cheek personality analysis.

The analysis is written purely to reflect the attributes and history of the chosen font but it has been surprising how closely people thought they reflected their own personalities. It has been interesting to talk to people about their font choices, and to hear what they think is so accurate about their 'fortune'. These have proved so popular that they now make a regular appearance at Type Tasting events.

Type Dating Game

"Is it fair that typography is seen as the least sexy design discipline?" Rob Alderson 'It's Nice That'[4]

To expand on the Font Fortunes idea I created the first version of an online Type Dating Game. This is a light-hearted, gamified survey created to encourage participants to think about the personalities of different fonts and which they identify with.

Players are invited to choose a typeface to represent themselves at a speed-dating event. They then go on to choose which fonts they would date, ditch and be just friends. Along the way they are asked why they are making some of the choices. The explanations, although written as if they are about people, build up a comprehensive impression of the different font personalities.

The names of the typefaces are only revealed at the end so the answers given throughout the game are based on the letterforms. Once they have chosen their final date participants receive a personality analysis both of themselves and of their date. Like the Font Fortunes game, these are also based entirely on the attributes of the typeface. When asked how accurate they thought the analyses were 48% answered 'very' to 'spot on', 38% said 'good' to 'fairly', with just 14% saying they were not accurate.

This is a fun way of exploring whether we pick typefaces that reflect our values and mirror our personalities. It is not particularly scientific, but it does demonstrate that we readily identify with fonts and that we instinctively know which ones we might be compatible with.

Turn the page if you would like to play the Type Dating Game. Which typeface will you be, and which will you date, ditch or just be just friends?

A selection of the results can be found on pages 96 – 99. At the time of writing 5,145 participants have completed the survey. The majority being non-designers from the UK and US.

Type Dating Game. Which font is your dating type?

You arrive at a speed dating event. Decide which
name badge best reflects you, choose carefully as
this will form everybody's first impression of you.

"Hello"
A

"Hello"
B

"HELLO"
C

"Hello"
D

"Hello"
E

"Hello"
F

"Hello"
G

"Hello"
H

"Hello"
I

Which badge do
you choose?

Why?

- - - - - - - - - - - - - - - - - - - -

- - - - - - - - - - - - - - - - - - - -

- - - - - - - - - - - - - - - - - - - -

- - - - - - - - - - - - - - - - - - - -

- - - - - - - - - - - - - - - - - - - -

- - - - - - - - - - - - - - - - - - - -

- - - - - - - - - - - - - - - - - - - -

First round

You meet your first three potential dates and chat to each for 60 seconds.
Think about their personalities. What qualities are you attracted to?
Who do you fancy?
The bell goes. It's time to fill in your scores to the right ...

DATE #1   **Date #2**   Date #3

Date: ☐
Ditch: ☐
Friend: ☐

Second round

You meet your next three potential dates
The bell goes. It's time to fill in your scores to the right ...

Date #4   *Date #5*   *Date #6*

Date: ☐
Ditch: ☐
Friend: ☐

Third round

You meet your final three potential dates
The bell goes. It's time to fill in your scores to the right ...

Date #7   **Date #8**   Date #9

Date: ☐
Ditch: ☐
Friend: ☐

Time to decide. Tick who you choose as your ultimate date?

#1 ☐   #2 ☐   #3 ☐   #4 ☐   #5 ☐   #6 ☐   #7 ☐   #8 ☐   #9 ☐

Why did you choose this person?

- -

- -

Turn to page 99 for the personality analyses.

Results: which typefaces do people choose to be?

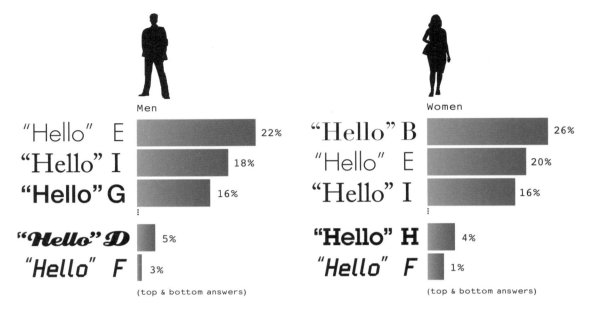

Men

"Hello" E	22%
"Hello" I	18%
"Hello" G	16%
"Hello" D	5%
"Hello" F	3%

(top & bottom answers)

Women

"Hello" B	26%
"Hello" E	20%
"Hello" I	16%
"Hello" H	4%
"Hello" F	1%

(top & bottom answers)

Why men choose to be E (Futura).

It's simple and easygoing. Slick. Simple and well-polished. Tasteful, modest, classic. Minimalist, but substantive. Elegant, legible. Practical, clear, elegant. Smart, simple, open, secure and true. Edgy, clean, smart. Serious, old school, simple. Genuine. Down-to-earth. Normal and standard. It shows power and class without arrogance. Low key. Quiet, unassuming. Shows a bit of interest and personality. A modern classic. Modern, slick, urbane, polished. Reserved and subtle. It's crisp and sharp looking, kind of like how I like to portray myself. It shows I'm no nonsense but still have a sense of humour. That I'm professional and interested in work but still have a sense of fashion. I am or at least want to be refined. Stylish and calm. Somewhat traditional, with a sense of style. Subtle, quiet...

Why men choose to be I (Caslon).

It's kinda serious, but not too serious. Kinda fun, rounded bit at the end of the 'y'. Classic, balanced, meritocratic. Bookish, intellectual, reserved but interesting. Very open and easygoing. Reserved, classical, serious, meticulous. Straightforward, but a touch a of flare. Intelligent. Classical elegance. It is straightforward, no-nonsense and classy. Traditional yet bold. Grounded, classy, clear. Classic, clear, simple but thoughtful, invites exploration. Uncomplicated without being plain. Clean, down to earth, no-frills. Clean, not overbearing, direct. Formal but not overly so, more like business/casual. Traditional with soft edges. I like to think I am clear and classic. Clean, classic, strong. Professional. Smart, reserved, and not desperately screaming for attention. Traditional, I like serifs because they help...

Why women choose to be B (Didot).

Serious and intellectual yet can be fun. I like beautiful classic things. Subtly classic. Fun & flirty, but stable & loyal. Calm, precise, clean. Sophisticated. Love of beauty, precision and intelligence. Classy, feminine, smart, stable. Sophisticated but sexy. To the point with flair. Classic. I think it's classy and elegant. Subtle self confidence. A little personal flare. Classic, not flashy. It's very measured. Honest, sense of humour. Elegant style. Very simple, fairly reserved. Easygoing, laid-back. Intelligent. It's elegant and differentiated. Classic, polished and elegant. Artsy but elegant. Serious, smart and stylish. It's simple and classic. Inviting, open. Interesting. Understated, elegant. Clear, no games, clean lines, nothing too extravagant or in your face, respectful. Different but still tasteful. Contrasts, thick/thin...

Why women choose to be E (Futura).

Neat and simple. It's round and organised and looks neat. Clear and straightforward. Sleek, crisp and to the point. It is a little unusual, contained and shapely. Simplistic and not too flashy. It's simple but sexy. Not fussy, clean, somewhat modern. Cute, clean, simple. Honest, classic. I am down to earth, but interesting. Easy, not intimidating. Simple, straightforward. Open and unpretentious, not 'in your face'. I want you to make your own impression without me telling you what it should be. Clean and crisp lines. Simple, no drama, minimalist. It's clear simple and classic but fun. Simple, easygoing. Minimal, clean, confident with a side of playful. Creative and honest. Clean and organised. Straightforward, not overly fancy. Open, simple, deliberate, clear. Clean, easy to read, pleasing, sophisticated. Classic...

The Type Taster

Results: which are the most dateable types?

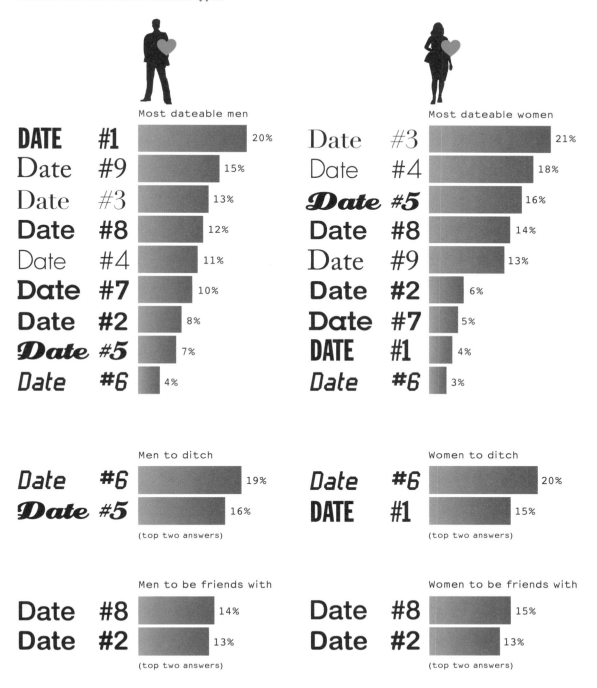

Most dateable men

DATE	**#1**	20%
Date	#9	15%
Date	#3	13%
Date	**#8**	12%
Date	#4	11%
Date	**#7**	10%
Date	**#2**	8%
Date	***#5***	7%
Date	*#6*	4%

Most dateable women

Date	#3	21%
Date	#4	18%
Date	***#5***	16%
Date	**#8**	14%
Date	#9	13%
Date	**#2**	6%
Date	**#7**	5%
DATE	**#1**	4%
Date	*#6*	3%

Men to ditch

Date	*#6*	19%
Date	***#5***	16%

(top two answers)

Women to ditch

Date	*#6*	20%
DATE	**#1**	15%

(top two answers)

Men to be friends with

Date	#8	14%
Date	#2	13%

(top two answers)

Women to be friends with

Date	#8	15%
Date	#2	13%

(top two answers)

Type Dating Game results. How the most dateable typefaces are described

Most dateable men:

Strong and masculine and well dressed. Friendly & easy going. Strong straightforward and bold. Good looking, smart, refined. The font is masculine and confident. Tall, bold, and can be fun. Not obtrusive. Looks romantic. A little out of the box, but not too much. Classic, gentleman, intelligent. Responsible, yet fun. Well-balanced, interesting, funny. Easy to get along with, not overbearing and good with almost any situation. He looks good in a suit & tie, or in jeans & a t-shirt. Can be serious & have fun. Attractive, funny, intelligent, decided, adventurous, masculine. Solid, bold. Sincere and normal. This person is both decisive and charismatic. Approachable, trustworthy. Bold and thorough, a good man as a role model. Strong yet not to serious. Looks smart and goal oriented. Hard working strong sexy manly great father great friend great lover. He seems like a good guy. Stands out, bold, strong. Attractive, well-rounded, interesting. Strong but artsy.

Masculine, easy to understand, classic, steady. Smart, with money, nice. Honest and sincere. He's bold, smart, confident. Confident. Kind. Honest. Strong straight forward and bold. Intelligent but not pretentious and not silly. Strong but not too bold. Serious friendly and reliable. I think he is intelligent, a manly man, a true gentleman, simple, I think we are different and it makes it interesting. Doesn't seem too serious, a bit interesting, and pleasing to look at. Seems most balanced between serious and fun. Stable. Understated charm. Friendly & easy going. He's classy and intelligent, but not arrogant. He is intelligent and kind and doesn't leave you guessing. Subtle, classic, gentlemanly, with enough of a modern twist to be adventurous. Stable, bold, daring, decisive. Fun, direct and smart. Intelligent, classy, clear. Honest and strong. They're straightforward, bold, and full of laughter. Traditional and cultured. Sleek minimalist style seems drama-less. Sturdy...

Most dateable women:

She is fun, sexy and casual. She is intelligent and stable. Quiet yet sophisticated. Elegant, attractive. Scholarly, professional, and feminine. Calm and beautiful. She looks fun! Seems trusting, has good feminine qualities, takes care of herself. She seems both trustworthy and interesting. Educated and sophisticated. Beautiful, cultured. Classical, a little flirty lots of stability and traditional. Classy, likes to dress up and go out nice. Classic elegance with style and substance. Beautiful, intelligent, slightly reserved. Sophisticated but sexy. A little untraditional, unshowy, simple. Probably best ballroom dance partner. She seems a bit quirky. Stable, classy, timeless, understated. Easy going, but also gorgeous. Exotic, sensual, fun and a little dangerous. Clean, Feminine, and might be fun to figure out a way to take out of her comfort zone. Sexy. She has a nice body, nice curves but also the right amount of 'muscle' in her bones. The skinniest one. Friendly, sophisticated, casual. Clean, classy, and modern. Stylish, but not begging for attention. Classic, beautiful and multifaceted. Classy. Curved, definite, bold. Kind of old fashioned, but still fun. Elegant, classy, feminine. She could be classy and stylish, elegant. Most stylish with good humour, cuteness, and pizzaz. Looks like a fun, outgoing, intelligent personality. The most feminine and approachable, friendly and companionable. Interesting conversation, classy tastes. Beauty. Fun sexy. I guess it was love at first sight. Seems modern, into pop culture and calm and collected. Good balance between fun, easygoing and serious, firm. most distinctive, intelligent, independent, and capable. Elegant, Understated, Classic, Stylish. Style, but a certain playfulness as well. I like a woman with style and acts feminine, doesn't try to be the man. She's fun. Unconventional, interesting, attractive. Clarity and elegance. Stylish, simple, intelligent, creative. Classic looking, simple, not overbearing. Sophisticated, elegant, classy. Airy, clean...

How accurate did people think their personality analysis was?

Very. Pretty correct. Pretty spot on. Somewhat. Accurate except I'm not that fancy. Not very accurate. VERY accurate!! 70%. scary :). Very. Pretty cool, but I love to entertain people tho. Very!. Not bad. Somewhat accurate. Not Even Close. Very. Somewhat. My analysis is right on! Cool and scary lol. Spot on. My date is exactly what I look for in a partner and I would like to think I'm a very relaxed and laid back person. Dead on. Accurate. Amazingly accurate on the potential date. This describes my husband to a 't'. Wow! Not very good at articulating at times, but otherwise accurate. Semi-accurate. VERY. 100% spot on for me! A little too spot on maybe! I am a Designer though I know Type!. It is mostly accurate for me but exact for my husband. Good. Scarily accurate. Not bad. Not sure. I think it was pretty good, maybe 90% accurate, fun survey!. Maybe 70%. I really like it. F***ing accurate!. Pretty accurate. I don't know how traditional I am. Perhaps with design, but not so much real life. ACCURATE!!!!!. Quite ok :). Fairly. My date is accurate, but my font isn't. 100%. Pretty accurate. Identical. My personality is right on! Kind of good. But I also kind of expected that answer. So a bit stereotypic, both from me and the game. Relatively!! Woah! Quite accurate about the 'extrovert on the outside, introvert on the inside' part, but I don't go to THAT many parties :P. 60%. Not particularly accurate. Quite true. 7/10. very, since I think I am a creative and artistic person and you mention these two similar words. Very accurate. Pretty accurate. Pretty good. 100%. Yes. Quite accurate, but 100%. Pretty damn cool. Very! scarily accurate!. !!!. 0%. I think that accurate, differs in some details, but cool nonetheless. I have no idea. Eh close. 100% correct. Fairly accurate, it was fun :). Very much accurate...

Type Dating Game. Personality analysis given out for each typeface

"Hello" A/Date #2

You are friendly and open, usually to be found with a welcoming smile on your face (when you get old you'll have smile lines not frown lines) You're less of an intellectual and more of an appreciator of all things sensory—from the taste of food to creating a comfortable environment. If friends need a comforting voice and a shoulder to cry on they usually turn to you. You chose **Arial Rounded bold** by Robin Nicholas & Patricia Saunders.

"Hello" B/Date #3

You relish the opportunity to dress up in style and go to a glamorous party. You enjoy fashion and are drawn to classic and European styles. You appear to be confident and outgoing but this hides your more reserved and possibly introverted personality. You think it's the small, finishing touches that reveal the most about a person. You chose **Didot** by Firmin Didot.

"Hello" C/Date #1

You have an alpha personality; you're confident and easily take the lead in any situation. You're comfortable taking centre stage but this will be for practical reasons; you're not here to entertain. What people don't always see is that you're actually

a big softie with a generous heart. Your family and friends are important to you and you're always there to protect them. You chose **Franklin Gothic bold condensed** by Morris Fuller Benton.

"Hello" D/Date #5

You are casual and laid back, far more comfortable in jeans, t-shirt and bare feet than suited and booted. You are drawn to slightly unconventional people who are often artists or creatives. You're not an organised clock-watcher, preferring that events unfold in their own time. You chose **Eclat** by Doyald Young.

"Hello" E/Date #4

You are stylish in your appearance, with a designer aesthetic. You speak openly and clearly, preferring to think things through and give a well-considered opinion rather than to just blurt out the first thing that comes to mind. Your home reflects your minimalist chic style. You chose **Futura light** by Paul Renner.

"Hello" F/Date #6

You are confident and assertive. You think quickly on your feet and are a dynamic go-getter in all things. You're most likely to by found in active settings

both in your work life and your leisure time. You get bored quickly. You like to win. You chose **Cinema Gothic** by FontGeek.

"Hello" G/Date #8

You like to appear neutral and to weigh up a situation before revealing your true personality. In social situations you're more of a chameleon than a peacock, preferring to fit in rather than to take centre stage. You chose **Helvetica** by Max Miedinger, Eduard Hoffmann.

"Hello" H/Date #7

You are confident and have your feet firmly planted on the ground. You're more of a doer than a thinker. Your opinions are well considered and you balance out the pros and cons, but at the end of the day you call a spade a spade. You chose **Lubalin Graph** by Herb Lubalin.

"Hello" I/Date #9

You have traditional values. Although first impressions may be that you are fairly conservative, people quickly discover that you are curious and inquisitive. You are well read and can always recommend a good book or two. You are also well travelled and have many stories to tell. You chose **Caslon** by William Caslon.

References
1 'Silent Messages: A Wealth of Information About Nonverbal Communication (Body Language)' by Albert Mehrabian, Professor Emeritus of Psychology at UCLA, kaaj.com.
2 'You Are What You Wear: What Your Clothes Reveal About You' by Dr Jennifer Baumgartner.
3 British Institute of Graphology, britishgraphology.org. Mehrabian poses the theory that when we talk 7% of what we communicate is through our words, 38% by our tone of voice and 55% by our body language.
4 It's Nice That, itsnicethat.com

The current Type Tasting 'Tested on Humans' surveys and workshops can be found at typetasting.com.

Sniff this
6

Sniff this
8

Sniff this
7

Sniff This
10

Sniff this
9

Sniff this
9

Sniff this
8

11

Sensory type

Sniff

10

Equipment from a Type Tasting session.

SENSORY TYPE

Having the ability to absorb information through multiple senses simultaneously speeds up our ability to judge situations and to react quickly when necessary. Neurobiologists Stein, Stanford and Rowland[1] suggest that this is fundamental to our ability to recognise signals and to communicate, and that this has played a vital role in human survival.

Today you live in a visually dominant world and almost half of your brain is involved in processing what you see; yet biologically you are built to use all of your senses to interpret your environment. For example, a large proportion of your genes are devoted to detecting odours which suggests that smell played a much more important role in your evolutionary past[2].

Training expert Dugan Laird[3] breaks down learning into 75% through seeing, around 13% from hearing and the other 12% is through touch, smell and taste if absorbed through individual senses. However, if more senses are stimulated at any one time the experience can become intensified and the learning is considerably more effective. Evoking multiple senses can be used as a powerful teaching tool and memory aid.

Your strongest memories are multisensory and this can be demonstrated by asking you to describe (out loud) a past holiday experience that sticks in your mind. You will most likely refer to more than one of your senses: what you saw, the temperature, what you touched and how it felt, what you could smell and often what you ate or drank.

Reading a printed book is a multisensory experience: you smell the paper, feel the texture and hear the pages as you turn them. After reading her first book on an eReader a friend told me that, although it was a good book it had somehow lacked impact and she felt like "the intensity had been turned down". She realised she had missed the tactile qualities of the paper.

Tasting the rainbow

"Why does the voice of the ventriloquist appear to come from the lips of his/her dummy?" asks Professor Charles Spence.[4] He explains that, not only does perception occur simultaneously across all of your senses, but what you experience in one sense can trigger a reaction in another sense (or 'sensory modality'). These are known as 'crossmodal' interactions. For example you see a colour and know what it would taste like, you hear water pouring and know what temperature it would be, a smell triggers the anticipation of a flavour, you know what a shape would feel like to touch, or how loud and shrill a font would sound. The quiz opposite demonstrates how automatically you do this.

taste sound sight *smell* **touch**

Sarah Hale tells of starting a new job working in a supermarket staff canteen.[5] An 'old hand' cook explained the recipes to her, including one for raspberry sauce made of sugar, water, cornflower and pink colouring. "But where's the raspberry?" Sarah asked, and says "a look of amazement stole over the cook's face as if this had never occurred to her. 'I dunno.' she said, 'it *tastes* of raspberry.'"

Some of your instinctive responses to shapes, taste and colour are "hardwired into your evolution" for your protection and survival according to beer expert Pete Brown.[6] For example fruit turns red and round when it is ripe to eat so you associate red and round shapes with sweetness. Many poisons are sour or bitter so your sense of taste has evolved to help you avoid these.[7]

You also learn associations from seeing type used on food packaging and in advertising. You know what indulgently decadent or low calorie fonts look like, which are cheap or expensive, and which are sweet or savoury.

Exploring the crossmodal potential for type, or 'sensory type', is something I am involved in researching on an ongoing basis. Some of the initial ideas and outcomes are shown in this book.

Synaesthesia

Approximately 1 in 2000 people have synaesthesia[8] and they experience senses that would usually be separate as linked together.[9] For example, a synaesthete might hear colours, see sounds as shapes, the number five might always be red or taste metallic. These are crossmodal experiences created by the brain that are unique to that person. Famous artists with synaesthesia include David Hockney and Vincent Van Gogh, Olivier Messiaen, Tori Amos and Duke Ellington.[10]

Forty-nine-year-old synaesthete Lisa Olliff only realised five years ago that the way she sees things is unique to her. She told me "I can't understand how others see things in their heads." When Lisa looks at months, days and letters they have colours, for example "July is bright green, October is white, H is yellow, Wednesday is burnt orange and K is green." She also sees the calendar in 3D and from different angles: "It's as if I am viewing from the side or as if I am on a train track, riding on it."

Graphic designer Jamie Clarke experiences synaesthesia as individual letters and numbers each having a "correct colour" and these are consistently the same. He says that this does not impede his graphic design work as the effect is "blotted out" once the characters are combined to create words or sentences.

Crossmodal research

At the Crossmodal Research Laboratory at Oxford University[11] Professor Charles Spence and his team research the links between words, shapes and flavours. They have proved that soft and round shapes are associated with sweet tastes and rounded sounds like the nonsense word 'maluma'. Jagged shapes taste sour and associate with harsh sounds like the word 'takete'.[12]

"takete"
SOUR

"maluma"
SWEET

They have found that these associations also apply to typefaces: the team have proved that an angular typeface (53 point *Hollywood Hills regular*) scores as tasting sour and that a rounded typeface (44 point *Swis721 BlkRnd black*) is rated as tasting sweet.[13]

Bitter/Sweet Typography

Sensory branding experts Condiment Junkie have undertaken research proving that specific sounds are linked to different tastes[14] and used this as the basis to compose soundscapes. Listening to these soundscapes whilst eating different food has been shown to intensify the experience of each taste significantly.[15]

Reading about this prompted me to wonder whether the same could be done with type; whether letterforms could be matched to each taste and we could ultimately create typefaces for bitter, salty, sour, sweet and unami. These are my initial explorations to provide a starting point.

Process

(1) I selected food known for each taste and ate it whilst listening to the appropriate soundscape. I filled a sheet of paper with abstract marks and shapes that visually represented the experience of each taste, shown on the right.

(2) I took the abstract marks and either sourced typefaces with similar visual qualities, or where a typeface did not already exist I either modified existing fonts or created new letterforms.

(3) To test out my results I created an online survey to see whether participants match the letterforms to the same tastes. I included images of food to prompt more accurate sense memories.

Results

The results of the online survey show most agreement with the 'sweet' typeface, and this bears out the original findings of the Crossmodal Research Laboratory. The other tastes show some but less significant agreement, so the next stage is to develop the shapes further and to test them in person with real food.

Future research

I am doing collaborative research with the Crossmodal Research Laboratory to explore this further. They test the proposed ideas under more rigorous scientific conditions; the first study is to be published shortly.[16]

Type Tasting online survey Bitter/Sweet

Sweet

Abstract marks   *Candice*

Salty

Abstract marks   New letterforms

Bitter

Abstract marks   Modified *Klute*

Sour

Abstract marks   New letterforms

Results (answers from 82 participants)

sweet	92%	salty	36%	bitter	38%	sour	39%
bitter	3%	sour	36%	sour	31%	bitter	33%
sour	3%	bitter	25%	salty	26%	salty	23%
salty	2%	sweet	3%	sweet	5%	sweet	5%

Still or Sparkling?

The team at the Crossmodal Research Laboratory investigated label designs on a range of still and sparkling water bottles.[17] They conducted a study that looked at both shape and colour on the labels and concluded that the shape is more important than colour for differentiating between the two types of water. An organic-shaped logo was consistently matched with the still water and the sparkling water was consistently matched with the angular-shaped logo (right). The team observed that these findings are not reflected in current water bottle label designs.

Organic

Angular

I became interested in exploring whether these findings could be applied to the typefaces used on water bottles, and the implications this could have for graphic designers in terms of the range of graphic language we use.

(1) Do rounded and angular typefaces match the experience of drinking still and sparkling water?

(2) Is it possible to create a scale of still to sparkling (calm to energising) typefaces?

Process

I created two online surveys in which participants compared typefaces and letterforms, indicating which they thought were more still or sparkling. After cross-referencing both sets of results I was able to create the still to sparkling scale on the right.

Results

Rounded typefaces are consistently matched to still water and angular ones to sparkling water. The most 'still' typefaces have balanced shapes, with no thick/thin contrast. This is more important than whether the letter shapes are curved or angular. The transition from still to sparkling can be broken down into five distinct stages.

Type Tasting Still or Sparkling? online survey.

Still   Sparkling

Sparkling (energised)

Sloping forwards, not flowing
Thick/thin contrast
Angular shape

water
Sloping forwards, not flowing
Moderate thick/thin contrast
Rounded and angular shape

water
Sloping forwards, flowing
Moderate thick/thin contrast
Rounded and angular shape

water
Balanced
Moderate thick/thin contrast
Rounded, organic shape

water
Balanced
No thick/thin contrast
Rounded, geometric shape

Still (calm)

Cheap and instant food packaging often appeals directly to the desires of your subconscious.

Further up the price range the typography on the packaging becomes more intellectual.

Judging a meal by its packaging

Today we rarely hunt for or gather our food in the wild: we purchase most of it which means that it is linked to decisions about which shops we go to and the brands we buy. According to design writer Steven Heller,[18] "food is culture, it is a code or symbol for class and social strata" and the packaging is designed to both appeal to and reflect your lifestyle. He comments that "we are what we eat" is a familiar phrase, but today "we are what we buy" would be more accurate.

In some instances the making of food choices as a lifestyle statement can even overshadow decisions about the nutritional value of the food itself. "From sophisticated choices to culinary camp, your choice of food proclaims your attitude towards life," says Catharine Weese.[19] We expect food to both entertain and nourish us and we effectively consume a meal twice: once in our imagination when we're in the shop and again later when we actually eat it.[20]

"The drama of the package will always give you a better appreciation of the product." Packaging designer Primo Angeli

Gastroporn

Cheap and instant food packaging often appeals directly to the desires of your subconscious. These are the instincts that are hardwired into your evolution. The food packaging entices you with curvaceously sweet looking letters, words written salaciously in melted cheese, or drizzled out of rich and creamy chocolate. The words are often in the shape of the food they describe so that the lettering does not just say cheese, it is cheese[21]. These designs tap into your primitive survival instincts, which drive you to search for sweet and calorific foods.

Further up the price range the typography on the packaging becomes more intellectual and you must refer to your mental database of learned associations. The type is generally more understated, often in traditional Roman Serifs, italics, light weight typeface styles and sometimes combined with handwriting or distressed effects to signify 'hand-made'. Generally, the more expensive, the more refined the type becomes. Packaging conventions vary from country to country so when you are shopping abroad where the shops are unfamiliar, you can end up with a few surprises in your shopping basket.

Haddock and chips

A: *Balega*

Haddock and chips

B: *Helvetica Neue thin*

Haddock and chips

C: *Gill Sans ultra bold*

HADDOCK AND CHIPS

D: *Gill Sans shadow*

Describe what style and price range of each meal on the left from the type.

A: --

B: --

C: --

D: --

Turn to page 108 to compare your answers to the key to food packaging type.

beer

We are used to seeing angular typefaces on beer labels.

Love it or hate it, the London 2012 typeface energised the Olympic Games that year.

We don't like triangles

The brain's fear processor, the amygdala, plays a key role in recognising potential threat.[22] It becomes activated by visual elements with angular or sharp contours and it remains unaffected by soft contours and round shapes. As a result we favour curve-shaped objects and this is called 'contour bias'.

Packaging designers are aware of contour bias and this is why most packaging features either curved letters or classic Serif/Sans Serif type styles. This is even the case on products like crisps where angular shapes and lettering might better represent the crunchy experience. Lettering styles are generally rounded and 'friendly' (although they might occasionally feature a triangle in the background of the design or in the logo).

Marketing psychologist Louis Cheskin was the pioneer in studying people's emotional response to packaging in the 1930s.[23] In his most famous experiment he found that 80% of people preferred a design with circles when given a choice between circles and triangles. Manufacturers are cautious of taking the risk that incorporating angular shapes or making any changes that might reduce sales.

In his book about hidden meanings in packaging, Thomas Hine[24] explains that designing packaging is a balance of getting a product noticed, but also having it accepted into people's homes. A design that is angular and attention grabbing in the shop may not convey the right emotional qualities once it is in the more peaceful domestic environment. Cheskin demonstrated that triangles are highly visible although "people can see them but that doesn't mean they like them". He found that circles and ovals are received most positively but they are found to lack personality on their own, and that they became more interesting when combined with angular shapes.

However contour bias only holds true for neutral objects and shapes and it is dispelled once you recognise the object. A hand grenade looks to be a safe, round shape but you have learned that it is dangerous, which overrides the amygdala's instinctive (lack of) response.

Designers and manufacturers could take more risks that would result in the typographic landscape of the supermarket becoming more interesting. We are used to seeing angular type styles on beer labels and—love it or hate it—the London 2012 typeface energised the Olympic Games that year.

Key to food packaging type (from Type Tasting online survey results)

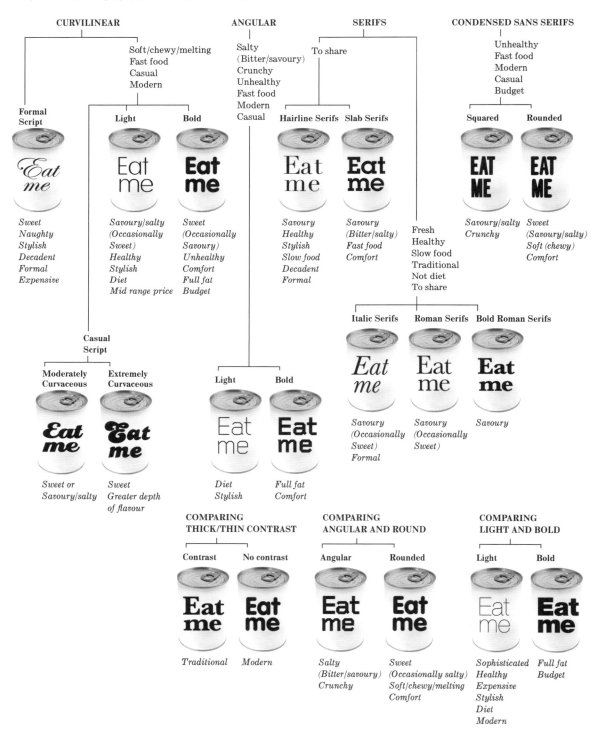

CURVILINEAR

Soft/chewy/melting
Fast food
Casual
Modern

Formal
Script

Sweet
Naughty
Stylish
Decadent
Formal
Expensive

Light

Savoury/salty
(Occasionally
Sweet)
Healthy
Stylish
Diet
Mid range price

Bold

Sweet
(Occasionally
Savoury)
Unhealthy
Comfort
Full fat
Budget

Casual
Script

Moderately
Curvaceous

Sweet or
Savoury/salty

Extremely
Curvaceous

Sweet
Greater depth
of flavour

ANGULAR

Salty
(Bitter/savoury)
Crunchy
Unhealthy
Fast food
Modern
Casual

Light

Diet
Stylish

Bold

Full fat
Comfort

SERIFS

To share

Hairline Serifs

Savoury
Healthy
Stylish
Slow food
Decadent
Formal

Slab Serifs

Savoury
(Bitter/salty)
Fast food
Comfort

Fresh
Healthy
Slow food
Traditional
Not diet
To share

Italic Serifs

Savoury
(Occasionally
Sweet)
Formal

Roman Serifs

Savoury
(Occasionally
Sweet)

Bold Roman Serifs

Savoury

CONDENSED SANS SERIFS

Unhealthy
Fast food
Modern
Casual
Budget

Squared

Savoury/salty
Crunchy

Rounded

Sweet
(Savoury/salty)
Soft (chewy)
Comfort

COMPARING
THICK/THIN CONTRAST

Contrast

Traditional

No contrast

Modern

COMPARING
ANGULAR AND ROUND

Angular

Salty
(Bitter/savoury)
Crunchy

Rounded

Sweet
(Occasionally salty)
Soft/chewy/melting
Comfort

COMPARING
LIGHT AND BOLD

Light

Sophisticated
Healthy
Expensive
Stylish
Diet
Modern

Bold

Full fat
Budget

The Type Taster

1933

Guns

Bold, large condensed
eg *Alternate Gothic*

Cigars

Bold, non italic, condensed
eg *Cheltenham condensed extra bold*

Moving pictures

Regular, large
eg *Caslon bold*

Typewriters

Non italic, small
eg *Century*

Golf clubs

Bold, medium, non italic
eg *Cheltenham bold*

Perfume

Non bold, regular or small, italic
eg *Goudy Old Style italic*

1935

Cheapness

Cheltenham bold

Dignity

Caslon

Luxury

Savoye

Strength

Cheltenham bold

Economy

Goudy

Automobiles

Caslon italic

Perfume

Savoye

Coffee

Goudy

Jewellery

Savoye

Building materials

Cheltenham bold

Type styles for historic commodities

"A typeface needs to be sympathetic to the product and to emotionally engage with the consumer." Michael Everett, copywriter

Some of the early research into typefaces was conducted in 1933 by psychologists R. C. Davis and Hansel J Smith at Indiana University.[25] In their study called the 'Determinants of feeling tone in type faces', the psychologists explain that they had observed statements like "bold type expresses cheapness", "italic types express femininity", and "Bodoni type expresses modernness" being made regularly but without proof. They set out to prove the validity of these claims, and to match fonts to a range of 1930s commodities from guns and typewriters to cigars and perfume as a guide for graphic designers and advertisers.

Two years later Gwendolyn Schillebi opened her report[26] in the 'Journal of Applied Psychology' with the statement: "Advertising is one of the most important fields to which psychology has been applied." In her study, 'An experimental study of the appropriateness of colour and type in advertising', participants were asked to match typefaces to abstract qualities like cheapness and dignity, and then to commodities like automobiles, coffee and building materials.

A selection of the results of both studies are illustrated above (typefaces have been substituted where the originals were not available).

Packaging design today is more sophisticated than it was a century ago in terms of both materials and design. However, taking into account that Sans Serif type styles were not yet in commonplace use in the 1930s, these examples show that typographic conventions remain fairly constant.

Wake up and smell the fonts

We interact with fonts either as professionals who actively use typefaces, or as type consumers on the receiving end.

Type professionals
A type professional is engaged in the process of consciously choosing and using type in their work and as a result they have a wide vocabulary to draw on. Non professionals can find this language intimidating and when I start conversations people will often begin with an apology like "I'm sorry I don't know anything about fonts." There is a general misconception that people need to be experts to have opinions.

Type consumers
As end users we encounter fonts as we go about our everyday lives. We generally 'look past the font' and interact with them unconsciously. We are all experts as type consumers; we all know instinctively how to respond to the different shapes and styles of fonts because we have been doing this all our lives. Fonts only communicate with us because we already understand their meanings.

In the film short 'Font Men'[27], type designer Jonathan Hoefler explains that he thinks there

is a "poverty of descriptive terms" for the experience of typography. He finds himself using phrases which are purely descriptive or that involve cultural references, like: "it's too Steven Segal and not Steve McQueen enough".

Part of what I do under the Type Tasting banner is to initiate conversations about the experience of typography from the type consumer's point of view. This involves getting away from the jargon and using the descriptive language of the consumer, which can range from discussing which fonts you would date to how they might taste or smell.

In a Type Tasting session participants are set challenges which include being asked to match jars of smells and bowls of food stuffs to a range of typeface samples. The debates that follow can be very lively and, although they are about taste, texture and smell, the language used sounds authentically typographic.

Answers
Page 102

Typefaces

Page 103
Five senses typefaces: *Candice, Shatter, Futura, Edwardian Script, Klute.*

Page 105
Still: *VAG Rounded*, sparkling: *Klute.*

Sparkling to still: *Klute, Cocon (Mateo, Cocon, Bodoni Poster italic), Cocon (Cocon, Bodoni Poster italic, Candice), Candice (Cocon, Bodoni Poster Italic, Candice), VAG Rounded.*

Page 107
Beer: *Fette Fraktur*, Olympics: *London 2012.*

References
1 'The Neural Basis of Multisensory Integration in the Midbrain: Its Organization and Maturation' by Barry E. Stein, Terrence R. Stanford, and Benjamin A. Rowland, 2009.
2 *The ICI Report on the Secrets of the Senses*, 2002, The Communication Group, London.
3 *Approaches to training and development* by Dugan Laird, 1985, Perseus Books.
4 'Crossmodal processing' by Charles Spence, Daniel Senkowski and Brigitte Röder, 2009, Crossmodal Research Laboratory.
5 'Flavour: there's a lot more to it than meets the eye. (Or tongue, or nose, or ears…)' by Pete Brown, 2013, petebrown.blogspot.co.uk.
6 Ibid Pete Brown.
7 'A Matter of Taste', by Society for Neuroscience, 2011, brainfacts.org.
8 'Everyday fantasia: The world of synesthesia' by Siri Carpenter, 2001, apa.org.
9 UK Synaesthesia Association, uksynaesthesia.com.
10 'List of people with synesthesia', en.wikipedia.org.
11 Crossmodal Research Laboratory, Department of Experimental Psychology, University of Oxford.
12 'The Sweet Taste of Maluma: Crossmodal Associations Between Tastes and Words' by Anne-Sylvie Crisnel, Sophie Jones, Charles Spence, 2012, Crossmodal Research Laboratory.
13 'Predictive packaging design: Tasting shapes, typefaces, names, and sounds' by Carlos Velasco, Alejandro Salgado-Montejo, Fernandon Marmolejo-Ramos, Charles Spence, 2014, Crossmodal Research Laboratory.
14 'As bitter as a trombone: synesthetic correspondences in nonsynesthetes between tastes/flavors and musical notes' by

Anne-Sylvie Crisnel, Charles Spence, 2010, Crossmodal Research Laboratory.
15 condimentjunkie.co.uk/blog/2014/6/20/bittersweet-symphony.
16 'The taste of typeface design' by Carlos Velasco, Andy Woods, Sarah Hyndman, & Charles Spence, 2015, Crossmodal Research Laboratory.
17 'On the colour and shape of still and sparkling water: Insights from online and laboratory-based testing' by Mary Kim Ngo, Betina Piqueras-Fiszman, Charles Spence, 2012, Crossmodal Research Laboratory.
18 'Food Fight' by Steven Heller, 1999, *AIGA* vol 17.
19 *Design as a Main Course* by C. Weese, 1999, *AIGA* vol 17.
20 'Eat your words, Food as a system of communication' by Sarah Hyndman, 2001, London College of Communication.
21 Ibid Sarah Hyndman.
22 'Visual elements of subjective preference modulate amygdala activation' by Moshe Bar and Maital Neta, 2014, *Neuropsychologia.*
23 *The Total Package, The Secret History and Hidden Meanings of Boxes, Bottles, Cans, and Other Persuasive Containers* by Thomas Hine.
24 Ibid Thomas Hine.
25 'Determinants of feeling tone in type faces' by R C Davis, Hansel J Smith, 1933, Indiana University.
26 'An experimental study of the appropriateness of colour and type in advertising' by Gwendolyn Schillebi, 1935, Barnard College.
27 'Font Men' by Dress Code presented by *AIGA*, 2014, vimeo.com.

The current Type Tasting 'Tested on Humans' surveys and workshops can be found at typetasting.com.

low calorie

Cooper Black / Helvetica light

STRONG & POWERFUL Strong & Luxurious

Flemish Script (Edwardian Script '&')
Helvetica condensed black oblique

FAST FOOD fast foode

VAG Rounded bold / Rubber Stamp

sweet

Candice / Modified Klute

W water

Klute / VAG Rounded bold

12

Everyman

Garamond / Gill Sans

Altered experiences

Relaxed

Mateo / Bodoni Poster italic

sweet

Cola

Gone

Monotype Script / Bauhaus light   *Klute / Aspirin*   *Candice*   *Drawn letters*

Klute

Experiment: Sweet and Sour

You need two matching fruit flavoured sweets—for example, jellybeans or fruit gums of the same colour.

Eat Me #1

Eat the first sweet while you look at the words 'eat me' above. Score how it tastes.

How sweet? (0 = not sweet, 10 = extremely sweet)

0	1	2	3	4	5	6	7	8	9	10
☐	☐	☐	☐	☐	☐	☐	☐	☐	☐	☐

How sour? (0 = not sour, 10 = extremely sour)

0	1	2	3	4	5	6	7	8	9	10
☐	☐	☐	☐	☐	☐	☐	☐	☐	☐	☐

ALTERED EXPERIENCES

Before reading this chapter take part in the Sweet and Sour experiment on pages 114 and 116.

"The truth about what you 'taste' is that most of it happens not in the mouth, but in the brain," explains beer expert Pete Brown after attending the Edinburgh International Science Festival's Sensory Dining dinner. Food and drink can be experienced without physically consuming them because taste is "just the firing of neurons".[1] This also means that your perception of what you taste can be influenced or altered by other factors. In other words, priming your expectations can alter the actual experience of the food you eat.

In his TEDx talk, Professor Charles Spence[2] explains that if you tell somebody that a bottle of wine is either £90 or £5, they will experience the £90 bottle as being more pleasurable to drink, even if it is the same bottle of wine. He says they will also find the aspirin they take the next morning

to be "significantly more effective" in reducing the symptoms of pain if they are told they cost £5 instead of £1.

"The drama of the package will always give you a better appreciation of the product." Primo Angeli[3]

The first time I experienced this altering of perception was at a demonstration by sensory branding experts Condiment Junkie.[4] The sound of a crackling fire was playing in the background and an image of pale tree trunks was projected across the wall as we drank a glass of whisky. It tasted deep and smoky. Then the sound of the crackling fire was changed to high, tinkling sounds and the trees were replaced by a deep red light. Suddenly, mid-mouthful, the whisky became sweet—all the smokiness had gone. They explained that they could alter a person's perception of what they tasted by up to 20% with colour, light and sound.

Dr David Lewis asked two groups to each read from one of two identically worded menus describing 'rich and creamy' tomato soup. The only difference was that one was written *Courier* and the other in *Lucida Calligraphy*. After eating the soup they were asked to rate it for taste, freshness and enjoyment. Lewis found that those who read the *Lucida Calligraphy* menu rated the soup as tasting 64% tastier, fresher and more enjoyable. Twice as many said were likely to purchase it themselves. The typefaces primed participants to have a better (or worse) experience of the soup.[5]

```
Rich &
Creamy
Tomato
Soup
```
Courier

*Rich &
Creamy
Tomato
Soup*

Lucida Calligraphy

The emperor's new packaging

In his work dating back to the 1930s, marketing psychologist Louis Cheskin[6] proved that the appearance of the packaging has a dramatic

VAG Rounded

Eat Me #2

Eat the second sweet while you look at the words 'eat me' above. Score how it tastes.

How sweet? (0 = not sweet, 10 = extremely sweet)

0	1	2	3	4	5	6	7	8	9	10
☐	☐	☐	☐	☐	☐	☐	☐	☐	☐	☐

How sour? (0 = not sour, 10 = extremely sour)

0	1	2	3	4	5	6	7	8	9	10
☐	☐	☐	☐	☐	☐	☐	☐	☐	☐	☐

The Type Taster

Ice Cream A

Ice Cream B

Ice Cream C

Ice Cream D

Ice Cream E

Ice Cream F

Ice Cream G

ICE CREAM H

Which is the sweetest? ____   Which is sorbet? ____   Most expensive? ____   Cheapest? ____

Low calorie? ____   Most rich and creamy? ____   Most appealing? ____

effect on the taste of crackers, soup and beer. He calls the transferring of the imagined experience promised by the packaging to the actual experience of eating the food 'sensation transference'.

How does packaging influence us without us being aware of it? Author Thomas Hine suggests "we are all so accustomed to looking past the package that we don't see it even when it is put right in front of our eyes". He explains that we experience a visual overload in a supermarket which we cope with by not consciously looking at everything but we "still see plenty" because we take it all in subconsciously.[7] According to packaging designer Primo Angeli packaging contains, protects, informs and advertises the food inside. It must stimulate a craving or hunger by "seducing our most primal urges". As food became increasingly mass produced from the 1800s, manufacturers saw the opportunity to use the packaging to encourage people to purchase their products. Today there is a huge amount invested in this specialist industry.

Tested on humans

What were your answers to the ice cream quiz at the top of the page? Generally sweet and rich and creamy foods are associated with curvaceous typefaces (A, D, F and G). Angular shapes suggest sour flavours like citrus sorbet (B). Light weight and ornate styles are considered to be more expensive E, G), whilst bolder and mechanical looking letter shapes appear cheap (D, H). The most appealing ice cream depends on your preferences. You may prefer a full-fat, brightly-coloured indulgence, or a palette-cleansing sorbet.

In a supermarket the 'low calorie' or 'healthy eating' options will often be represented by light weight typefaces like example E (see page 108). The skinny letters and all the space around them represent the reduced calorie content at a glance. However, when I buy them I already know that I will likely still feel hungry at the end of the meal. I buy them because I ought to, not because I have been seduced into wanting to. Since the packaging sets up expectations that influence the eating experience, I would like the healthy option to convince me it will be satisfying to eat.

The 'Sweet and Sour' experiment on pages 114 and 116 is based on a Type Tasting demonstration I give. At a recent event I gave the 100 members of the audience two jellybeans to eat, both the same colour and flavour. One was eaten whilst looking at angular-shaped letters (page 114) and the other whilst looking at a round shaped typeface (page 116). Both were in black on white so it was just the typeface that was changed so the results were not affected by colour. The audience rated the sweets eaten to the jagged-shaped letters as tasting 11%

sourer, and the identical jellybeans eaten to the round typeface as tasting 17% sweeter. The type actually altered how the sweets tasted.[8]

The results are similar every time I do this experiment. How do your answers compare?

I have also done this experiment with crisps, which have seemed to taste saltier and crunchier. These demonstrations are designed to be theatrical rather than scientific. However, this area is being researched by the team at the Crossmodal Research Laboratory under scientific conditions whose findings bear out the results. Looking at different shapes, whether these are logos or typefaces, can alter our perception of taste. This effect can be amplified once colour, shape, texture and photography are included.

Placebo fonts

We live in a time when obesity, diabetes and heart disease are reaching catastrophic levels and society is becoming increasingly post culinary[9] as we cook less and consume more pre-packaged food. According to the UK government "in England, most people are overweight or obese including 61.9% of adults and 28% of children aged between 2 and 15"[10]. The UK government has policies on reducing obesity and improving diet which are actively encouraging businesses to "reduce ingredients (for example salt and fat) that can be harmful if people eat too much of them".[11] 'The Consensus Action on Salt and Health in the UK' proposes that the food industry reduces the salt content of all foods by 50–60% over the next five years.[12]

It has been proved that we have the power to influence the taste of food because the packaging sets up expectations that can alter how the food tastes. Could this be used for good? Could we add sugar, salt and fat to food via the packaging, like a placebo, and reduce the amounts in the actual food? But do this so that our perception of what the food actually tastes like is unaltered?

Research is currently underway into the use of multisensory illusions to enable levels of sugar, salt or fat in food to be reduced without altering the perception of the taste.[13]

Typefaces
Page 117
Ice cream A: *Cooper Black*, B: *Cinema Gothic*, C: *Balega*, D: *VAG Rounded*, E: *Helvetica light*, F: *Candice*, G: *Flemish Script*, H: *Impact*.

References
1 'Flavour: there's a lot more to it than meets the eye. (Or tongue, or nose, or ears...)' by Pete Brown, 2013, petebrown.blogspot.co.uk.
2 'Expectations of pleasure and pain' by Professor Charles Spence, 2014, TEDxUHasselt.
3 *Upscale, Downscale: We Are What We Eat* by Ellen Shapiro, 1999, AIGA vol 17.
4 'The Singleton Sensorium' by Condiment Junkie, condimentjunkie.co.uk.
5 *The Brain Sell, When Science Meets Shopping* by Dr David Lewis.
6 *The Total Package, The Secret History and Hidden Meanings of Boxes, Bottles, Cans, and Other Persuasive Containers* by Thomas Hine.
7 Ibid Thomas Hine.
8 Typetasting with Sarah Hyndman and Design Week, London Design Festival at the V&A, londondesignfestival.com.
9 'Eat your words, Food as a system of communication' by Sarah Hyndman, 2001, London College of Communication.
10 'Policy: Reducing obesity and improving diet', 2013, gov.uk.
11 Ibid gov.uk.
12 Committee on Medical Aspects of Food, Recommendations made about salt, 1994, actiononsalt.org.uk.
13 *The ICI Report on the Secrets of the Senses*, 2002, The Communication Group, London.

The current Type Tasting 'Tested on Humans' surveys and workshops can be found at typetasting.com.

Could type be used to make food healthier?

IMAGINED

Placebo

Nutrition Facts

Total Sugar 28g	9%
Actual Sugar 23g	
Imagined Sugar 5g	

Placebo

Nutrition Facts

Total Salt 0.53g	9%
Actual Salt 0.43g	
Imagined Salt 0.1g	

ADDITIVES

Imaginary **sweet**

Imaginary *salty*

Imaginary crunchy

13

Edible type

Helvetica water biscuits with rosemary.

EDIBLE TYPE

I have found turning type into food to be an effective way of initiating conversations about the experience of typography using evocative and descriptive language and which often provokes lively debates. A discussion about, for example, what *Times New Roman* would taste like or what kind of cheese *Helvetica* would be still sounds authentically typographic.

Some recipes draw on the provenance of the typeface and involve researching its origins. This is a great way to teach and learn about type history. Alternatively, they take the type consumer as the starting point and represent the experience of interacting with typefaces.

Tasting packs

These were originally created to celebrate Type Tasting's first Christmas. Each contained three typefaces interpreted as food along with a chocolate-box style description sheet.[1]

Impact Helvetica, *Comic Sans*

The 'Eye' magazine team reviewed a pack, judging each typeface on its taste, texture, letterspacing and suitability. A few of the team's comments are included here and the full review can be read on the 'Eye' blog.[2]

Impact: **Dark chocolate laced with chilli**
Impact is a Sans Serif display typeface with ultra-thick strokes and compressed letterspacing. It was designed by Geoffrey Lee in 1965 for attention-grabbing headlines. The dark chocolate with chilli version is bold and packs an in-your-face punch.

"Great, *Impact* should be dark with a kick." Jay Prynne

"The richness of the dark chocolate and the spicy hit of the chilli makes an impression on the tastebuds." Sarah Snaith

Helvetica: **Savoury biscuits**
A Neo Grotesque Sans Serif typeface designed for neutrality which has achieved ubiquity. It was developed in 1957 by Max Miedinger with Eduard Hoffmann. It has been cooked up as simple, savoury biscuits with little flavour of their own which can work with any topping.

"Practical and safe with no surprises." Janet South

"Would have been nice with cheese." Jay Prynne

Comic Sans: **Candy melts with popping candy**
Vincent Connare created the Casual Script that people love or hate for Microsoft in 1994. As the name suggests it is inspired by comic book lettering. *Comic Sans* has been interpreted as brightly coloured, extremely sweet chocolate-style candy filled with popping candy.

"Sweet with undertones of guilty pleasure." Simon Esterson

"*Comic Sans* deserves better." John L. Walters

Helvetica

Recipe: *Helvetica* water biscuits with rosemary[3]

Helvetica was designed to be highly readable but neutral. It was intended to be an invisible carrier of words that added no additional meaning of its own through the shape of the letters.

The edible interpretation of Helvetica reflects this in the form of savoury water biscuits that are plain enough that they can be topped with any food without influencing its flavour. They have a sprinkling of salt and a dash of rosemary for a Swiss Alpine touch.

The biscuits are cut out using 3D printed cookie cutters. Alternatively you could use a printout of your selected letters as a stencil to cut around.

Serving suggestion: A menu staple which is good to have in the cupboard for everyday snacks and meals. Best served with cheese, cold meat or a tasty dip.

Ingredients

200g plain flour
1 tsp baking powder
50g butter, cut into cubes
2 tsp dried rosemary
Sea salt

Method

Preheat the oven to 175C/350F/Gas 4. Prepare baking trays by greasing them and lining with non-stick baking paper.

1. Mix the flour, baking powder, butter, rosemary and 1/2 tsp of the sea salt until the butter is mixed in with the flour.

2. Add 4 tbsp water and mix until the dough comes together. If it feels dry add more water and process until the dough is soft but not sticky.

3. Roll out the dough on a floured work surface as thinly as possible. The thinner the better.

4. Cut out your biscuits using either the biscuit cutters or templates you prepared earlier.

5. Place on the baking tray. Brush water over the surface of the dough, sprinkle a little salt over the top. Prick the biscuits with a fork.

6. Bake for 10–15 minutes until the biscuits feel dry but are still pale. Place on a wire rack to cool.

Baskerville

Recipe: *Baskerville* Earl Grey tea biscuits[4]

Baskerville is a Transitional Serif typeface created by printer and type designer John Baskerville in the 1750s. It is a recognisably English typeface that has stood the test of time as a legible, everyday text face.

Baskerville was created at a time when improved technology and transport enabled new and exotic foods to be imported and tea become the 'national drink'. The edible interpretation of *Baskerville* is as Earl Grey tea biscuits for an authentic 18th century flavour.

The biscuits are cut out using 3D printed cookie cutters. Alternatively you could use a printout of your selected letters as a stencil to cut around.

Serving suggestion: These are elegant biscuits with depth of flavour, making them versatile enough as a snack or for more formal occasions. Best served with a pot of tea.

Ingredients

200g butter
200g caster sugar
2 tsp finely ground Earl Grey tea leaves (use decaffeinated tea for less of a caffeine hit)
1 large free-range egg, lightly beaten
400g plain flour

Method

Preheat the oven to 175C/350F/Gas 4. Prepare baking trays by greasing them and lining with non-stick baking paper.

1. Cream the butter and sugar with the finely ground tea using a wooden spoon. Add the egg and beat until combined. Add the flour and mix until the mixture forms a dough.

2. Gather the dough into a ball, wrap it in cling film and chill in the fridge for an hour.

3. Roll out the dough on a floured work surface to approx 0.5cm thick.

4. Cut out your biscuits using either the biscuit cutters or templates you prepared earlier.

5. Place on the greased and lined baking tray. Wash with beaten egg and sprinkle with tea.

6. Bake for about 8 minutes until golden brown. Place on a wire rack to cool.

Burlingame

Recipe: *Burlingame* **pick 'n' mix sweets**[5]

Monotype, together with The Massachusetts Institute of Technology (MIT), conducted an exploratory study[6] into type styles which would minimise a driver's glance time when looking at in-vehicle displays. They found that Humanist Sans Serif typefaces with distinctly different letterforms were the most effective. The findings of the study inspired the typeface *Burlingame* that was designed by Carl Crossgrove

The edible version of the typeface recreates the flavours of a long car journey to represent the inspiration behind *Burlingame's* design.

Coffee and mint liquorice style caramels

Half of the letters are created out of liquorice style caramel for the tactile feel of a car's black leather or plastic dashboard. This is flavoured with coffee and mint for the 'stay awake' journey experience of service station take-away coffees and mint sweets.

Zingy lemon jelly letters

By contrast the illuminated numbers and letters are made from lemon jelly sweets. The zingy lemon contrasts with the deep coffee flavour and they shine brightly against the dark liquorice.

Serving suggestion: Wrap the sweets individually and serve from pick 'n' mix bags for motorway service station authenticity. Ideal served up on long car journeys.

The sweets were originally created to celebrate Monotype reaching 5,000 Twitter followers. The full recipe can be found on the Type Tasting blog[7].

Edible history of type

Blackletter was the first printed type, created in Germany in the 1450s and based on the meticulous handwriting of scribes (see page 47).

I suggest this could be the hors d'oeuvres served at the beginning of a typographic banquet, which would take guests through the history of type with each course. It starts with the beginnings of print and the meal ends with a dessert inspired by fantastical ideas for the future of type made possible by developments in technology.

'Gutenberg Bible' hors d'oeuvres

An ornate illuminated letter made of spiced meat and pickled fruit arranged on a slice of rye bread. This is ancient bread which was a staple in Germany in the 1400s. 'Sliced bread' also functions as a metaphor for mechanical reproduction made possible by printing process.

The meat and fruits are to be laced with medieval spices and natural food colouring to bring the sculptural illuminated letter to life, and the pages of the book are printed in a Blackletter style typeface with edible ink to look like a page from the 'Gutenberg Bible' (above).

Eat your words

I often ask people what they think fonts would taste like. BBC Three Counties Radio presenter Nick Coffer[8] thinks *Comic Sans* would be "rocky road chocolate mousse with over-sickly marshmallows on the top and a bit of a dusting of icing sugar, perhaps with some glacé cherries". London taxi driver Akin suggests *Times New Roman* would be a "full English breakfast" because it is a filling version of an everyday meal, just like 'The Times' newspaper.

Birmingham City University students Edna Ma and Ian Nguyen proposed *Courier* to be a sushi roll, the equal spacing between each letter mirroring the monospaced typeface.

Fellow student David Hansel suggested *Didot* would taste like classic French macaroons with a raspberry and buttercream filling.

What typeface would you cook up and what would it taste like?

Cooking up a batch of *Futura*

Doughnut alphabet by Karina Monger

Processed cheese extra bold on rye

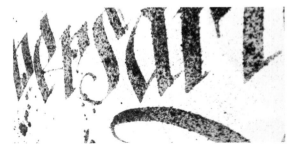
Chilli and soy sauce calligraphy by Alice Mazzilli

References
1 'What does type taste like?' by Sarah Hyndman, 2014, typetastingnews.com.
2 'Type on the tongue', Eye Magazine blog.
3 'Helvetica water biscuits recipe' by Sarah Hyndman, 2014, typetastingnews.com.
4 'Baskerville Earl Grey tea biscuits recipe' by Sarah Hyndman, 2014, typetastingnews.com.
5 'What would Monotype's Burlingame typeface taste like?' by Sarah Hyndman, 2014, typetastingnews.com.
7 Ibid Sarah Hyndman.
6 'Monotype Introduces the Burlingame Typeface Family', press release by Monotype, 2014, monotype.com.
8 'Talking 'fonts'' on BBC Three Counties Radio, 2014, typetastingnews.com.

The current Type Tasting 'Tested on Humans' surveys and workshops can be found at typetasting.com.

drink me

drink me.

Eat Me

Diet food

Eat Me

Instant

EAT ME

economy

Eat Me

Decadent

PHRENOLOG

BY

L.N. FOWLER

INTUITIVE,
REASONING, REFLECTIVE,
FACULTIES.

LITERARY,
OBSERVING, KNOWING,

Appendices

Bodoni
Miracle Font

FORTUNE TELLER
Bauhaus
Miracle Font

FORTUNE TELLER
Gill Sans
Miracle Font

FORTUNE TELLER
Caslon
Miracle Font

Equipment and materials from Type Tasting events.

Tested on Humans: Type Tasting experiments and surveys

Much research done into typefaces explores readability and focusses on the mechanics of letter forms and how they function. I am interested in how we respond to them emotionally. To find out more about this it has been important for me to talk to a wide range of people. As well as organising events, inventing games and asking lots of questions I have created an ongoing series of Tested on Humans surveys and experiments.

Initially these began as a way to test out the assumptions I make as a graphic designer such as whether everybody recognises similar personalities in typefaces? To do this I paticularly wanted to find out from non-designers how they respond to typefaces in their role as type consumers.

I am interested in using these experiments as a fun way start conversations and to dispel the preconception that typography is a 'dry' subject for academics and experts. Typography is expressive; it is what our voices look like and it is how we express language visually. It reflects our everyday lives from highbrow to popular culture and the way we talk about it can reflect this cultural range.

Type Tasting surveys are intended both to gather information and to start conversations. Most are accessed via the Type Tasting website, although some are run from other places where they have no apparent links to typography.

The surveys collect a great deal of data, but they are not run under strictly scientific testing conditions. The intention is to highlight potential areas for future study in collaboration with scientists. This is currently being undertaken with some of the ideas initiated in the surveys.

Font Census (pages 80–85)
What personality types are different fonts? Participants are randomly assigned a font to answer questions about.
Each font has received 250–350 responses to date.

Emotions (page 66, 71)
What emotions do we see reflected in different letterforms and typefaces? This is an entry level survey aimed at non-designers.
Nearly 2,000 participants to date.

Eat Me (pages 104, 108, 110, 114, 116–118)
A range of surveys exploring what letterforms would taste like as food, and which investigate the visual codes of type on packaging design.
Various surveys both online and at events.

Font Fortunes (pages 89, 92, 93)
Are your values and aesthetics mirrored in the fonts you choose? Participants select from a range of options and receive a fun personality analysis based on the typeface they chose. They are asked how accurate they think the analysis is for their personality.
This demonstration is run at Type Tasting events.

Jellybean Demonstration (pages 114, 116, 117)
Can looking at different typefaces alter the taste of the jellybeans?
This demonstration is run at Type Tasting events.

Mood (pages 66–69, 71)
Various surveys include questions about the mood created by different typefaces and the results are cross referenced.
Various surveys.

What Type of Pub? (pages 18, 53, 133)
This survey matches pubs to fonts and asks what type of establishment you think each would be from the style of the typeface.
Over 300 participants to date.

Sounds Like? (pages 39–41)
These surveys explores what typefaces would sound like. Some involve wearing headphones and matching sounds to fonts.
Over 500 participants to date.

Still or Sparkling? (page 105)
Which typefaces appear most sparkling, or energetic, and which are more still or calming? The aim of this survey was to identify the features in a typeface that energise or calm it.
Over 500 participants to date.

Bitter/Sweet (page 104)
This is an ongoing project exploring whether different tastes can be represented as specific typefaces.
170 participants to date.

Type Dating Game (pages 93–99)
Participants are asked to choose a typeface to represent themselves for an evening at a speed dating event. They then select the type they would date, ditch and just be friends. This explores whether we see personalities in typefaces that reflect our relationships with the people around us.
Over 5,000 participants to date.

Font Census breakdown of three typeface personalities in detail, from page 81

Garamond — 316 responses

Helvetica — 336 responses

Bauhaus — 265 responses

The Visionary
The Artist
The Rebel
The Inspirer
The Idealist
The Performer
The Jester
The Commander
The Thinker
The Intellectual
The Wise Sage
The Monarch
The Doer
The Everyman
The Nurturer
The Leader

Type Tasting online survey results: What type of pub? Also see the 'What type of pub?' quiz on page 53

Didot: noisy, posh, wine bar, afterwork drinks, coffee and alcohol, sophisticated, above average income, City workers.

Copesetic: art deco, cheeky, expensive, cocktails, bistro, women, gin, glitzy, wine bar, prohibition, small glasses, big prices.

Engravers' Old English: ye olde English pub, proper boozer, long established, dimly lit, beer, ale, traditional, tavern.

Copperplate: country pub, open fire, traditional, warm, touristy, gentrified, next to a law court.

Flemish Script: fancy, dated, posh, a bit pretentious, middle aged, brandy, expensive, older crowd, champagne.

Trajan: upmarket, over-priced, wine bar, refined, civilised, traditional, stuffy, polite, decent, formal, good food, chain pub.

Buffalo Gal: rustic, saloon, new western, country music, tattoos, burgers, whisky, dive bar, denim, good for brunch.

Amelia: older people, theme bar, Beatles' tribute bar, funky, fruity cocktails, cheap, kooky, hippy, classic rock, 60s bar.

Cooper Black: seaside resort, retro, bargain boozer, warm beer, arcade machines, cheap, pre-drinking venue.

Times New Roman: pub for intellects, bland, boring, after-work crowd, chain pub, gin and tonics, not expensive.

Braggadocio: inner city, casual, retro, young, hotel bar, cool, cocktails, airport, quirky, bright colours.

Mesquite: peanuts, tequila, hazy saloon, stuffed animals, whiskey, bikers and old men, Americana, spirits, country music.

Helvetica: cheap, minimal interior, basic and bland, community, moody bar staff, cheap decor, metal furniture, cash only.

Fette Fraktur: heavy metal music, seaside pub, all beards, pie, ale, small town, bitter, German beers, dark and smoky.

Comic Sans: juice bar for kids, coffee, cheap food, backpacker hostel, this wouldn't exist, basic drinks, uncool.

Caslon Titling: meetings, town, lawyers, doctors, expensive, a hidden drunk, wear a suit, sophisticated, classical music.

Onyx: gastro pub, high class, pretentious, loud, cocktails, dancing, expensive club, smoking area, quirky, attractive exterior.

Stencil: hole-in-the-wall dive, outskirts of a town, cheap, student, drink all you can, grunge music, happy hour, cheap shots.

Terminology and anatomy

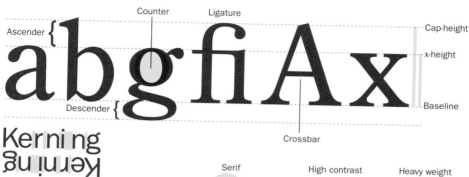

Ascender · Counter · Ligature · Cap-height · x-height · Descender · Baseline · Crossbar

Kerning
Kerning
Compressed
Stretched

Serif · High contrast · Heavy weight
Sans Serif · No contrast · Light weight

Double-storey · Single-storey

Display type:
Headline
Body copy
Lorem ipsum dolor sit amet, consectetuer adipiscing elit, sed diam nonummy nibh euismod tincidunt ut laoreet dolore magna aliquam erat volutpat. Ut wisi enim ad minim veniam, quis nostrud exerci tation ullamcorper suscipit lobortis nisl ut aliquip ex ea commodo consequat.

Ranged left
Lorem ipsum dolor sit amet, consectetuer adipiscing elit, sed diam nonummy nibh euismod tincidunt ut laoreet dolore magna aliquam erat volutpat. Ut wisi enim ad minim veniam, quis nostrud exerci tation ullamcorper suscipit lobortis nisl ut aliquip ex ea commodo consequat.

Ranged right
Lorem ipsum dolor sit amet, consectetuer adipiscing elit, sed diam nonummy nibh euismod tincidunt ut laoreet dolore magna aliquam erat volutpat. Ut wisi enim ad minim veniam, quis nostrud exerci tation ullamcorper suscipit lobortis nisl ut aliquip ex ea commodo consequat.

Centred
Lorem ipsum dolor sit amet, consectetuer adipiscing elit, sed diam nonummy nibh euismod tincidunt ut laoreet dolore magna aliquam erat volutpat. Ut wisi enim ad minim veniam, quis nostrud exerci tation ullamcorper suscipit lobortis nisl ut aliquip ex ea commodo consequat.

Justified
Lorem ipsum dolor sit amet, consectetuer adipiscing elit, sed diam nonummy nibh euismod tincidunt ut laoreet dolore magna aliquam erat volutpat. Ut wisi enim ad minim veniam, quis nostrud exerci tation ullamcorper suscipit lobortis nisl ut aliquip ex ea commodo consequat. Duis

Ascender
Extends above the x-height.

Body copy
The main section of text to be read in a printed or online document (see above right).

Calligraphic
Influenced by hand writing.

Cap-height
The height of the capital letters.

Centred (see above right).

Contrast
The contrast between the thick and thin elements of type.

Counter
The space enclosed within a letter.

Crossbar
Horizontal stroke.

Descender
This extends below the baseline.

Display Type
For large headlines (see above right).

Double-storey (see above).

Font
Traditionally a particular size, weight and style of a typeface (see page 27).

Glyph
An individual letter, character or symbol.

Italic
A cursive alphabet that slopes to the right.

Justified (see above right).

Kerning
The spacing between pairs of letters.

Leading
The spacing between the lines of text (separated by pieces of lead in traditional printing).

Ligature
Two or more letters combined to create a single glyph.

Monospaced
The width of all letters is the same and they are spaced out equally.

Pixels
Unit of measurement on screen.

Point (size).
Unit of measurement in print.

Ranged left (see above right).

Ranged right (see above right).

Sans Serif
'Without' serifs.

Serif
With serifs.

Single-storey (see above).

Type
All characters or letters that are printed or shown on a screen.

Typeface
A particular design of type (page 27).

Typography
The art of arranging type.

Weight
How light or bold a font is.

x-height
The height of the lowercase letters. Note the curved letters will sit slightly outside.

The Type Tactor

Type classification* (See note over the page)

BLACKLETTER >>

 Old English

 Fraktur

 'Fairy tale'

SERIF >>

 Roman inscriptions

 Humanist (Venetian)

Old Style (Garalde)

Transitional

 Modern

 Fat Face

 Condensed

Decorative

 Slab Serif

Typewriter

Decorative

 Engraved

 Glyphic (Flared)

 Tuscan

 Decorative

SANS SERIF >>

 Grotesque

 Humanist

 Neo Grotesque

 Geometric

Bauhaus

Art Deco

De Stijl

SCRIPT >>

Formal

Casual

Art Nouveau

Painted

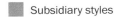 Major categories

Subsidiary styles

Blackletter
The first printed styles that emulated the handwriting of monks and scribes.

Humanist (Venetian) Serif
The first printed roman typefaces inspired by the handwriting of Italian Renaissance scholars.

Old Style (Garalde) Serif
More refined letterforms, many of which are still popular today.

Transitional Serif
They have a more robust vertical axis, sharper serifs and show the transition from Old Style to Modern.

Modern (Didone) Serif
Improvements in technology and paper quality made it possible to print the extremely fine details in these typefaces.

Slab Serif
Typefaces with heavy serifs that became popular for headlines, billboards and posters.

Engraved
Inspired by engraved lettering.

Glyphic (Flared)
Often considered to be based on letters carved in stone, the flared shapes of these letter are also created naturally by the flow of the sign writer's brush.

Grotesque Sans Serif
These are the early Sans Serifs that look a little like Serif typefaces but with the serifs removed.

Humanist Sans Serif
These have a hand drawn feel to their shapes. If you try to draw a Sans Serif letter in freehand it will most likely reflect the flowing contours of Humanist curves.

Neo Grotesque Sans Serif
These were the first Sans Serif typefaces to become commercially popular and are associated with the Swiss Modernist movement and with minimalism.

Geometric Sans Serif
These are based on geometric forms. They are considered to be less readable than Grotesques because the letter shapes look so similar.

Formal Script
This style of script is based on the handwriting of master calligraphers such as George Bickham and George Shelley.

Casual Script
These are informal letterforms that appear to have been written quickly. It is a popular sign writing style in the US.

References

* From page 135. 'Many design scholars have published various techniques of classification of typography. Most notably in 1954 Maximilien Vox introduced a classification of type, which was later adopted by the Association Typographique Internationale (ATypI)[1]. This rigid classification system was designed prior to the mass computer-generated type design age and therefore did not allow for the evolution and variation of digitally designed typefaces we have today. However it has been a beneficial tool to review type design evolution in a chronological order. For the purpose of this publication I have simplified the classification to 'Major categories' and 'Subsidiary styles''.

1 This would later be set as British Standards Classification of Typefaces (BS 2961:1967).

Typefaces

Sources

Photographs

All photos and illustrations are by Sarah Hyndman, unless credited otherwise.

Find out more

Stories about fonts/typefaces

'Design Museum Fifty Typefaces That Changed the World' by John L Walters (Conran).

'Just My Type: A Book About Fonts' by Simon Garfield (Profile Books).

'Type: The Secret History of Letters' by Simon Loxley (I.B. Tauris).

Creative lettering and type

'The 3D Type Book' by FL@33, Tomi Vollauschek and Agathe Jacquillat (Laurence King).

'Typography Sketchbooks' by Stephen Heller & Lita Talarico (Thames and Hudson).

'Typoholic: Material Types in Design' by Viction Workshop (Victionary).

Lettering and type in the environment

'Signpainters' by Faith Levine (Princeton Architectural Press).

'Signs: Lettering in the Environment' by Phil Baines & Catherine Dixon (Laurence King Publishing).

'The Field Guide to Typography, Typefaces in the Urban Landscape' by Peter Dawson (Thames & Hudson).

Typography

'Thinking with Type' by Ellen Lupton (Princeton Architectural Press).

'The Anatomy of Type: A Graphic Guide to 100 Typefaces' by Stephen Coles (Harper Design).

'Type and Typography' by Phil Baines & Andrew Haslam (Watson-Guptill).

'Stop Stealing Sheep and find out how type works' by Erik Spiekermann & E.M. Ginger (Adobe Press).

'The Geometry of Type' by Stephen Coles (Thames & Hudson).

'Typography' by Gavin Ambrose & Paul Harris (AVA Publishing).

Advanced typography

'An Essay on Typography' by Eric Gill (Penguin).

'The Elements of Typographic Style' by Robert Bringhurst (Hartley & Marks Publishers).

Crossmodal

'The Perfect Meal: The multisensory science of food and dining' by Charles Spence and Betina Piqueras-Fiszman (Wiley Blackwell).

Websites

'Eye' (International Review of Graphic Design) eyemagazine.com

Ghostsigns archive ghostsigns.co.uk

'Grafik' grafik.net

'I Love Typography' ilovetypography.com

It's Nice That itsnicethat.com

St Bride Library www.sbf.org.uk/library

Typographica typographica.org

Watch 'Wake Up and Smell the Fonts' by Sarah Hyndman at TEDxBedford

tedxtalks.ted.com/video/Wake-Up-and-Smell-the-Fonts-|-S

Mentioned

BBC Radio 4 bbc.co.uk/radio4

Crossmodal Research Laboratory psy.ox.ac.uk/research/cross-modal-research-laboratory

D&AD dandad.org

Laurence King Publishing laurenceking.com

London College of Communication (University of the Arts) arts.ac.uk/lcc

London Design Festival londondesignfestival.com

Pick Me Up Somerset House somersethouse.org.uk

South by Southwest sxsw.co.uk

TED/TEDx ted.com

Victoria and Albert Museum vam.ac.uk

With Relish withrelish.co.uk

Thank you

Cheerleaders Theo S, Miho A, Syd H, Zoë C, the Paragon gang, Luke G, Alexandra B, Alex F, Claire M, Hazel G, Becky C, Caryl J, Gaynor M, Natalie C, Helen R, Andy J, Minna O, Sarah L-K, Beverley G, Nicky M and Rona S.

Emily Gosling, Angus Montgomery, Emma Tucker and John L. Walters for taking me seriously. The Monotype team for taking me "just seriously enough".

Eagle-eyed Caryl Jones, Vinita Nawathe, Theo Stewart, Geraldine Marshall and Eugenie Smit.

Volunteers Chelsea Herbert, Emily Bornoff, Eugenie Smit, Eunjung Ahn, Eva Gabor, Lissy Bonness, Lucy McArthur, Lucy Pendlebury, Martin Naidu, Miho Aishima, Nicola Yuen, Paul Fine, Peter Strauli, Qian Yuan, Syd Hausmann and Zoë Chan.

Live letterers extraordinaire Oli Frape and Ruth Rowland. Everybody who took part in the exhibition and workshops at the V&A.

Makers of edible type especially Alice Mazzilli, Andreja Brulc, Christine Binns, Julie Muaro, Karina Monger and Stephen Boss.

The knowledgeable signpainting crew led by Sam Roberts, Ash Bishop, the inimitable Mike Meyer and his Brushettes.

Professor Charles Spence, Andy Woods and Carlos Velasco Pinzon.

Sarah Batten for your encouragement and patience.

To future type explorers Leon and Stefan, enjoy the journey.

Thank you to Monotype for the fonts.

Your cover choice personality analysis

This book is available with five different typeface options on the front cover. Here are the personality analyses of each cover choice.

the type taster

Cover choice:
Baskerville

You have traditional values and can be a bit of a perfectionist at times.

You prefer an intellectual or academic conversation over a display of emotions. Your style is of quiet refinement and you are the opposite of ostentatious. You are seen as wise and a little conventional but you are forward thinking and not old fashioned.

You read a great deal and enjoy a well-made cup of tea.

Your friends trust you to give well-informed and considered opinions, and that if you don't know the answer you'll just say so (rather than making something up).

Secret guilty pleasure: enjoying the smell of quality when you unwrap something new like a wallet or a handbag.

Baskerville is a Transitional Serif typeface which was designed by John Baskerville in Birmingham, England in the 1750s.

the type taster

Cover choice:
Clarendon

You have that quiet, assured confidence that means you do not have to shout to get attention. You are a natural leader although you do not always choose (or want) to be.

You have both feet firmly on the ground and have a love of the outdoors. You enjoy wide, open spaces and the freedom that comes from walking in the countryside.

You are a practical person and if there's a problem you would prefer to work out how to solve it yourself rather than delegating the task to others.

You are more of a doer than a thinker and all your views are your own.

Secret guilty pleasure: enjoying a nostalgic moment like crying at a sentimental film in the dark.

Clarendon is a Slab Serif typeface that was created by Robert Besley in England in the 1850s.

the type taster

Cover choice:
Didot

You come across as poised and thoughtful and this sometimes gives you an air of importance. However, this outward appearance of confidence hides your more reserved personality. You are a people watcher but, rather than doing this from the shadows, you are happy to stand in the middle of the room and to be seen.

You always know exactly how to dress for a situation, whether it is the glamour of a party or a casual weekend away.

You think it is the small, finishing touches that reveal the most about a person.

Secret guilty pleasure: doing something indulgent and messy like eating chocolate in the bath or wearing flip flops in the mud.

Didot is a Modern (or Didone) typeface. It is based on typefaces created by Firmin and Pierre Didot in Paris in the late 18th and early 19th century.

the type taster

Cover choice:
Gill Sans

You are a traditionalist who likes to think of yourself as being modern.

You are articulate, and you use the correct spelling and grammar in emails, texts and tweets—no abbreviations or acronyms from you. But this does not mean you are overly formal, far from it in fact. Your friends see you as an everyman (or woman), a regular Joe, one of the gang.

You have a cheerful, outgoing demeanour with a slightly idiosyncratic manner (which can occasionally frustrate those closest to you).

You are practical and you always know what to do in a situation so you will often be the person people turn to when they have a problem or need advice.

Secret guilty pleasure: swearing.

Gill Sans is a Humanist Sans Serif typeface designed by Eric Gill in England in the 1920s.

the type taster

Cover choice:
Helvetica

You are practical and versatile, and able to turn your hand to many things. You have a pragmatic and calm approach, which may give the impression that you are conventional and not a risk taker.

You like to take a neutral viewpoint and weigh up a situation before voicing a well-considered opinion. You will often find yourself as the mediator in a heated situation.

You are a minimalist at heart and feel happiest living in an uncluttered environment, ideally with views that stretch all the way to the horizon.

Secret guilty pleasure: dressing up for a stylish event, or an outlandish fancy dress party. You will give the impression that you need to be coerced into this, but secretly you really enjoy it.

Helvetica is a Neo Grotesque Sans Serif. It was originally created by Max Miedinger and colleagues in 1957.

The type taster: How fonts influence you
Written and designed by Sarah Hyndman

Published by Type Tasting
Limited first edition of 2,000
© 2015 Sarah Hyndman

Type Tasting
typetasting.com
Twitter @TypeTasting
Facebook /TypeTasting